SPRINGBOARD

QUICK CREATIVE ACTIVITIES TO LAUNCH LEARNING

Mary Beth Campbell

Carolyn Hill

Micah Jacobson

Published by:

Wood 'N' Barnes Publishing
2309 N. Willow, Bethany, OK 73008
(405) 942-6812

1st Edition © 2009, Wood 'N' Barnes Publishing
All rights reserved.

Cover Art by Blue Designs
Copyediting & Layout Design by Ramona Cunningham
Photographs by Belinda Ranstrom, Micah Jacobson, and Judy Cogan
Special thanks to the Quincy High School 2009 Business Technology students of Quincy, MA; students of Ithaca High School, Ithaca, NY; and students at the Belmont Student Link Conference (Notre Dame Belmont Academy, Tamalpais High School, Sonora High School, Bellarmine College Prepartory, Bret Harte High School, Ygnacio Valley High School, Holy Names High School, Moreau Catholic High School, and Milpitas High School).

Printed in the United States of America
Bethany, Oklahoma
ISBN # 978-1-885473-78-3

Acknowledgements

We would like to acknowledge and thank the community of Link Crew and WEB coordinators that have been our students, our teachers, and our inspiration in the work we do. They exemplify the spirit of working hard to create positive change in the world.

Play is vital to all humanity.
It is the finest system of education known.
Neville Scarge

Contents

The art of teaching is the art of assisting discovery.
Mark Van Doren

Introduction

Why Activities?

We are firm believers in creating experiences for students. Whether students are in a traditional classroom environment learning English, math, or history, or in another learning environment from science camp to Sunday school, we believe experience forms the backbone of learning. Why? Simply because creating as many hands-on learning opportunities as possible for students brings a level of energy, excitement, and authenticity to a classroom that cannot be replicated in any other way.

Regularly engaging students in this manner is the best way to get students to not only learn the material, but to feel it and process it as well. Studies show that it is not enough for students to just hear material in order to acquire the information; for students to really "get it" they must connect with it in an emotional way, have it resonate within their current schema, and draw new conclusions and formulate opinions based on that experience.* Experienced based learning is the perfect vehicle to enhance students' learning.

Furthermore, using activities in the classroom can create a lesser-known, but equally important, byproduct that is integral to the success of all students: a sense of community. Student success has been proven to be directly and significantly affected by the level of community and comfort students feel in the classroom.* Student success is greater when those in the classroom know and relate to each other, and activities can help students make these connections. Whether you are doing an activity that involves the whole class or is just a pair share, using activities in your classroom essentially creates the need for students to know each others' names, communicate effectively, and work together toward the accomplishment of a common goal.

Why Another Activity Book?

This book has been created in response to the many teachers with whom we have worked over the years who asked us to gather

---

* See Appendix A

some of our collective knowledge of activities and put it all in one place. As the cocreators and trainers of the internationally recognized Link Crew and WEB programs, we have stumbled upon and created numerous activities in support of our middle school and high school transition programs. Because these activities are also at home in classrooms of all kinds, we had many requests to put them in book form and offer them as tools to use for teaching.

Who Can Use This Book

This book assumes the reader has a basic level of awareness in regards to setting up, facilitating, and debriefing activities in the classroom. It also assumes there is an understanding of the "whens" and "whys" of doing activities within curriculum. So, if you are looking for a book that will give you the best ways to build activities into your curriculum, instructions on how to be an effective facilitator, or full lesson plans for each of these activities, this is NOT the book for you.

This book is a resource catalog of great activities that we have found to be: 1) fun to play, 2) thought provoking, 3) effective in communicating a concept, and/or 4) all of the above. These are activities that we continually use because they are some of the best we have found for accomplishing these goals.

How to Use What's in This Book

For the most part, the intent of this book is to provide experiences that will become a "springboard" for learning. They are designed to be as at home in a traditional classroom as they might be in an alternative setting. By and large, the activities we have selected for this book are meant to be short. That is, most of them do not take much time to set up, play, and debrief. While a few of the activities could be a class period unto themselves, many of them are meant to be used in combination with your curriculum. The book is divided into two sections: Engagers and Activities.

Engagers

What they are: These are short, usually goofy and silly, and don't take much set up. There are two kinds: in-seat and whole class.

Who can do them: They can be done alone, with a partner, or with the whole group.

Where to do them: Either in seats or a larger open space.

When to do them: Engagers are great for getting the class up and moving, loose and laughing. They are also perfect for demonstrating a point or initiating a discussion when you don't necessarily have a lot of time for a full blown activity.

How to use them: Build an engager into your lesson plan if you know you are going to need one at a certain point. Use them in that spontaneous teachable moment, when the moment has come, and when, for whatever reason, the time to do it is right now! This means, of course, that you should spend some time browsing through the engager section, committing a few to memory.

Activities

What they are: While activities can still be fun and silly, they generally take longer, require a bit more set up, and are designed, for the most part, to be used within the context of a larger lesson plan.

Who can do them: They can be used with any combination of people—pairs, 3 or more, large groups.

Where to do them: Activities require either a cleared classroom space or an outdoor space.

When to do them: Use an activity to help students discover or dissect a concept, or to create a common experience that can be related back to and discussed within the context of your curriculum. They are also great for having fun with your students when you have the time within your lesson plan.

How to use them: While activities are designed to be a part of a larger lesson within a unit, they can certainly be used in the same way as an engager (for movement and laughter), if time permits.

Creating Meaning

Read this section!

The activities in this book are designed to be conversation starters for discussion and interpretation around larger themes; essentially, they are springboards to learning. In daily life, we learn through our experiences. With each experience, we create meaning and walk away with either a thought we did not necessarily have before or reinforcement of an idea or thought we already held.

As educators, we have the opportunity to purposefully use activities in the classroom to generate a learning experience for our students. Sometimes, however, offering the experience alone is not enough to guarantee that learning will happen. Students need to be able to process and analyze their experience in order to see the meaning that it holds. Allowing your students the time and space to examine what happened during the activity gives them a greater chance to find meaning in it rather than walking away from it thinking that it was "just a game." While some students can and will do this kind of processing on their own, conscious processing facilitated by an educator makes a huge difference and can dramatically enhance learning outcomes.

Many activity books list a series of questions for the facilitator to use to guide the processing after an activity. You will not find questions like that following the activities in this book. Instead, we are providing you with an open-ended and comprehensive questioning model that will work not only for the activities in this book, but for any experiential activities you lead in your classroom. The reason we do not list activity-specific questions is because we would like to assist you as an educator in developing your style for extracting meaning from experience. Rather than tell you the appropriate questions for each activity, we have provided you with Activity Notes that will give you a general direction that might be useful to pursue. The **Activity Notes** combined with the following **Quick Start Guide to Questioning** will give you enough ground to start and room to grow.

Sometimes educators will use activities with a preconceived outcome in mind or for the purpose of delivering a specific message.

There is definitely a time and place for that kind of discussion. The challenge with that approach, however, is that students might discover their own meaning during the course of an activity. That meaning may be decidedly different from the educator's intent, thus making the student feel "wrong" in the debrief because their interpretation did not necessarily match what was being "taught."

This more directed style of debriefing can be effective and is sometimes necessary based on 1) available time, 2) the group with which you are working, and/or 3) the educator's purpose for using the activity. This style of debriefing, however, can also sometimes stymie real, true dialogue, as it might constrain students from actively engaging. It might appear that the learning to be gleaned from the discussion seems predetermined by the educator. Our intent is to expand the opportunities for true discussion and exchange of ideas through the questioning model below. We think it is important to the learning process that there are times when we don't "tell" students what they should learn through their own experiences, but rather that we ask them to discover that learning for themselves. It is the educator's job to help the students connect the learning they uncover to themselves and the subject matter that is being taught.

Quick Start Guide to Questioning

For every activity in this book, The 5 Questions* that follow can be used as a guide to process the experience:

1. Did you notice . . . ?

2. Why did that happen?

3. Does that happen in life or school?

4. Why/Where/How does that happen? (used in any order and as often as makes sense)

5. How will you use that to learn, grow, or change?

---

* The 5 Questions are excerpted with permission from *Open to Outcome: A Practical Guide for Facilitating & Teaching Experiential Reflection* by Micah Jacobson and Mari Ruddy, © 2004 Wood 'N' Barnes Publishing, 800-678-0621.

These 5 questions allow students to go through the learning cycle after any experience, and they help educators facilitate the discovery of meaningful insight for the students.

The Necessity of Observation

The beginning of a rich discussion depends on observation, either on the part of the educator or the students. The 5 Questions model puts the direction of the conversation in the hands of the educator starting with the initial question, "Did you notice...?" The remainder of the questions allow for vast interpretation and conversation that could essentially go anywhere.

The first question, "Did you notice...?" is purposefully incomplete and relies on the educator to fill in the sentence with an observation he/she made as the activity was happening. The more interesting and provocative the observation, the more dynamic and powerful the learning is likely to be.

The best way to initiate a powerful discussion is to pay close attention to your students as they experience the activity you are facilitating. What causes conflict? What challenges them? What might they be thinking or feeling? When it comes time, ask the "Did you notice...?" question with genuine curiosity and openness. Give the students a chance to look at that observation and what it means for them, without the filter of what you think or believe it means or should teach them. When used in conjunction with The 5 Questions, activities can truly be springboards to powerful "aha" moments in your classroom.

"I used these questions this past year to teach my Freshman English students how to research through the scientific method. It was a shot at getting them to choose research topics through observation as well as develop a skill that they will need to use in their Freshman Earth Science class. It worked like a charm. I would run activities such as Fast Fingers or Change Something and have them take observation notes, then we would make generalizations based on what we observed. I had no idea where it would go, but it led to amazing topics on gender issues, sibling rivalry, and peer pressure. All the while, they are playing."
Krista Gypton, 2008 Arizona Ambassador for Excellence in Education

How The 5 Questions Work in the Context of an Activity

Let's take the activity "Three Letter Body Parts" and see how an educator might use The 5 Questions to guide the learning process. In this activity, students are asked to create a list of 10 body parts with 3, and only 3, letters in the correct spelling. A common experience for many students is to get 5 or 6 and then get stuck. However, when the class works together, they are easily able to get 10 or more. The following is an *extraordinarily simplified* version of a processing conversation that might take place after this activity:

> Educator: **Did you notice** that when you were working on your own, many of you were able to think of only 5 or 6 body parts?
>
> Student: Yes.
>
> Educator: **Why** do you think that was?
>
> Student: Because we just couldn't think of them.
>
> Educator: **Does that ever happen in school or life** when you just can't think of everything or do everything by yourself?
>
> Student: Yes.
>
> Educator: **Where** does that happen, can someone give me an example?
>
> Student: Yeah, like when we are doing an assignment; sometimes I can't do the problems by myself, and I need help from the teacher or someone else in my class.
>
> Educator: Knowing that sometimes happens in school, **how** could we learn from this to be better students?
>
> Student: Well, when it's appropriate, we can seek help from others.

Obviously this is a fictitious and oversimplified conversation. In reality, students' comments move around, and they don't always answer the questions clearly. Sometimes they aren't sure what we are driving at as educators so they give the answer they think we want to hear. They want to get it "right" without really thinking about the questions we are asking. However, as you use The 5 Questions more, it becomes easier and easier to guide students toward their own learning.

When using The 5 Questions, it is important to note that with the exception of the first question (which should always be used to start the conversation), the questions need not be asked in a linear fashion. In fact, based on a student's answer, it may be best to re-ask one of the questions to either clarify or dig deeper into the conversation. You also might find the conversation going nowhere despite your best attempts. In that case, just start the process again with another observational "Did you notice...?" question. Following is a more complex conversation based on the same activity and the same initial observation as previously used. Notice that although the same observation is used, it leads to a completely different conversation, based on the educator's skill in using The 5 Questions:

Educator: **Did you notice** that when working on your own, many of you were only able to name 5 or 6 body parts?

Student: Yes.

Educator: **Why** do you think that was?

Student: Because we just couldn't think of them.

Educator: **Does that ever happen in school or life**; that you just can't think of everything or do everything by yourself?

Student: Yes.

Educator: **Where** does that happen? Can someone give me an example?

Student: Yeah, like when we are doing an assignment, sometimes I can't do the problems by myself, and I need help from the teacher or someone else in my class.

Educator: **Why** is it that sometimes you need help and other times you don't?

Student: Well, sometimes I need help if I don't understand a concept or if I missed class because I was sick.

Educator: **Why** might you not understand a concept that was taught in class?

Student: Like I said, if I was sick and missed class, or just didn't get it when it was taught.

Educator: Let's assume you were in class, **why** wouldn't you "get it?"

Student: Maybe the teacher didn't do a good job of explaining it, or maybe I wasn't paying attention.

Educator: **Does that happen sometimes in school**, that you don't pay attention in class and miss key concepts?

Student: Sometimes.

Educator: **Why** is that?

Student: 'Cause maybe I'm bored or don't like the class or the teacher or I don't understand the subject very well.

Educator: **How** can not paying attention in class, regardless of the reason, impact you?

Student: Well, I guess I'd get in trouble maybe, and my grades might go down because I wasn't getting all the information I needed to be able to do the work.

Educator: It seems that not paying attention in class can potentially have a negative impact. Knowing that, **how** can we use that information and learn from it?

Student: Well, I guess one thing we could do is figure out why you are not paying attention in class and address it. Like if you don't understand the subject, try to get help. If you don't like the teacher or the class, figure out what to do about it instead of just not doing anything. I guess, no matter what, you should do something to try and get yourself back on track.

As you can see, the same observation led to a completely different conversation with an entirely different outcome based solely on the educator's finesse with The 5 Questions.

For a full description of The 5 Questions, refer to *Open to Outcome: A Guide to Facilitating and Teaching Experiential Learning* by Micah Jacobson and Mari Ruddy. For a more in-depth guide to processing in general, we suggest *The Processing Pinnacle: An Educator's Guide to Better Processing* by Steve Simpson, Dan Miller and Buzz Bocher and *Tips & Tools: The Art of Experiential Group Facilitation* by Jen Stanchfield.

Structure of the Engagers/Activities

The activities listed in this book are all structured in the same way. The intention is that teachers will be able to pick up the book, flip to an activity, and use it with students five minutes later. Alternatively, we encourage you to look carefully through the book and gain an understanding of each activity. This will make it easier for you to pick out and use the activity that most perfectly fits the lesson plan you are creating. Look for these basics as you thumb through the activities:

Engager/Activity Title: The name of activities is somewhat arbitrary. While certain activities have very common names, others have been adapted, changed, or simply learned differently. Feel free to change the name of an activity if it will improve your lesson.

Possible Themes*: These are the themes that we consistently find in the activity. They suggest possible conversations an activity could inspire. This by no means implies that these are the only topics that can be used for these activities. In fact, as you play or set up the activities, you may find surprising and interesting lessons that we never saw! Themes, therefore, are a guideline to get you started. They should not be read as the only themes possible in an activity.

Supplies: We have worked hard to keep the number of supplies needed to a minimum. Many activities require no supplies at all. The following is a complete supply list for every activity in the book. If you have the following supplies on hand, then you can truly run every activity!

- Lots of blank paper
- Pens or pencils
- Dollar bill
- Chairs
- 5 dowel rods: 1 inch in diameter, 3 feet long
- Deck of cards

---

* See Table 1: Possible Themes for Engagers (pgs. 116-117), and Table 2: Possible Themes for Activities (pgs. 118-119).

- Backpack/daypack
- 4 or 5 heavy books
- Masking tape
- 1 inch sticky dots in 4 different colors
- 2 tubes of toothpaste
- 2 paper plates

Physical Set-Up[*]: There are a few different physical set ups required for these activities. They include:

Chair Circle: A circle of chairs with no barriers in between. Just circling desks won't work in these activities. You will need actual chairs and space to put them in a circle with nothing blocking the way.

Classroom: A traditional classroom set up with rows of desks all facing one direction.

Open Space: (Just what it seems.) Open space with no obstructions is required. Sometimes these activities can be done outside, but be careful of distractions that can take away from the focus of the activity.

Pairs: Students will be in partners, usually facing each other. They can stand in aisles or you can have open space. This structure is generally pretty flexible.

Standing Circle: Students should be in a circle facing each other with no obstructions between them.

Teams: Groups greater than two. The number of people in these activities can be flexible, depending on your needs. In fact, many of the activities listed as "pairs" can also be successful in groups of 3 or 4!

Do This or Say This: The instructions for this book are divided between things you do to set up the activity and things you say to give your group the instructions they need. Again, the intention is to make it as easy as possible to get your group playing.

---

* See Table 3: Physical Set Up for Engagers (pg. 120), and Table 4: Physical Set Up for Activities (pg. 121).

Of course, the "Say This"/"Do This" instructions are only guide-lines. We encourage you to adapt the language and make it your own. Just be careful not to miss the crucial instructions in any given activity.

Activity Notes: This section is where we talk about everything else. Often this area lists options, possibilities, and conversation start-ers. These notes are not meant to be exhaustive, but rather quick thoughts to give you some guidance in running the activities. **It is important to read the Activity Notes before you run any activity.**

Quick and Creative Ways to Partner

Several of the activities in this book require forming partners. Forming partners can and should be an activity in itself which, when done well, increases the connection and feeling of safety among participants.

The one process that we never like to see is the old, "Okay, every-one partner up with someone you don't know." This inevitably creates a number of undesirable outcomes. Students generally find friends and some are left out in the process. The few people who take the directive seriously could be opening themselves up to rejection from their peers. The process can take longer than it should, and instead of increasing community feeling, it ends up increasing feelings of exclusivity.

Following, you will find some of our favorite ways to create partner-ships and teams. These are meant to be starter ideas and once you get the idea of creatively partnering people, there is no limit to using these strategies.

Quick Partner: This is a way to partner at the beginning of the year or program that allows you to come back to the same partner over and over. Quick Partners is a wonderful way to establish pair-ings in a somewhat random environment. The basic instructions are the same for each of the creative greetings and once you under-stand the concept, there is an endless variety of partners you can create. Two examples follow:

High Five Partners: Say something like, "Everyone quickly find a partner, someone close to you, just grab someone quickly. Okay, this is your 'Hive Five' partner. Whenever I tell you to find your high five partner, you will find this person, give them a high five, and say 'High Five'!" (Always demonstrate the action you want your participants to execute.)

Lumberjack Partners: Say something like, "Okay, everyone quickly find a partner, someone close to you, just grab someone quickly. This is your 'Lumberjack' partner. Whenever I tell you to find your lumberjack partner, you will find this person, 'saw lumber,' and sing 'I'm a lumberjack, and I'm okay.' 'Sawing lumber' involves one of you giving the 'thumbs up' sign. Your partner then grabs that thumb, stacking their fist on top of yours. You then grab their thumb and so on until all four of your and your partner's hands are stacked up. Then the partners push and pull back and forth, simulating a saw."

With the same basic set up, imagine partnering for the following:

- High Low Partners
- Jedi Partners
- Fish Partners
- Bowling Partners
- Dosey Do Partners

Find Someone Who... : This partnering strategy directs the participants to the person who will be their partner. The criteria you choose will either create random groups or self-selected ones. There is a big difference in the partnership of people who have the same last digit in their phone number and those who like the same kind of music. Set a time limit, and when that time is reached, have remaining students grab the closest partner-free person. Have students find someone who meets the following criteria:

- Has the same number of siblings.
- Has the same last digit in one of their phone numbers.
- Likes the same toppings on pizza.
- Is wearing the same color shirt.
- Plays the same sport (or plays no sport).
- Likes the same kind of music.
- Has the same favorite subject in school.

Create a Team That... : Use this strategy for partners or groups of 3 or more. The goal is to give students a "team" or "partner" criteria that they need to meet. This is similar to "Find Someone Who..." but gives a greater degree of flexibility to students. Simply tell the participants to create a team or a partnership that collectively meets one of the following criteria.

- Has all colors of the rainbow represented in their clothing.
- Has a total of 5 siblings.
- Each likes a different genre of music.
- Each has a birthday in a different month.
- Whose total age is 39 (or whatever number will work for your group).
- Whose total height is under 12 feet (or whatever number will work for your group).

Mad Scramble: With the entire group in a circle, let them know that in a moment they are going to find a partner. They will only have 5 seconds to run into the middle of the circle, grab someone and return with them to the outside of the circle. Ready, set, go!

Pop Up: This strategy takes a bit of time and can help you create very purposeful partnerships. Have the group sit facing you, either in chairs or on the ground. Tell them that when you name a criteria, their job is to pop up quickly and look for someone else who popped up. Once they see that person, they must cry out in their most enthusiastic voice, "I knew it would be you!" The two then become partners, sit down together, and no longer pop up. The following are some ideas for criteria or invent your own, based on the group's needs.

Pop up if you:

- Were born in December (or any other month).
- Are not wearing shoes with laces.
- Have an e-mail account that includes your actual name.
- Still believe in the tooth fairy.
- Cry during movies.
- Were ever a girl or boy scout.

Engagers

To be playful and serious at the same time is possible, in fact, it defines the ideal mental condition.

John Dewey

Boom

Possible Themes: Synchronizing, continuous improvement, focus

Supplies: None

Physical Set-Up: Pairs

Do This

Have the group get into pairs. Have all the pairs stand or sit facing each other.

Say This

This activity is called "Boom." The goal of this activity is to synchronize with your partner. There are four simple motions that you need to learn. Let's practice each one together: Both Thumbs Up, Both Thumbs Down, Both Thumbs Left, Both Thumbs Right. Got it?

Okay, now face your partner. Starting slowly, clap once and then move your thumbs in one of the four motions. Clap again, and choose a different thumb motion. Continue to repeat this pattern: Clap – thumbs – clap – thumbs, keep it going, nice and slow...

Now let's stop for the final directions. Having figured out the "clap – thumbs" rhythm, you are ready to play with your partner. As you and your partner engage in that rhythm, look for the times when you both make the same thumb motion. When you make the same thumb motion, then instead of making a thumb motion after the next clap, you will clap, point at each other with both index fingers, and say "Boom." Then continue the game. For instance, it might look like this:

Person 1	Person 2
Clap	*Clap*
Thumbs Up	*Thumbs Right*
Clap	*Clap*
Thumbs Down	*Thumbs Down*
Clap	*Clap*
Point, "Boom"	*Point, "Boom"*
Clap	*Clap*
Thumbs Right	*Thumbs Left*

Activity Notes: At first, students may be tempted to match their partner's motions. It is important to point out that the goal of this activity is actually not explicitly matching or not matching. The goal is to develop a rhythm and pay close enough attention to your partner and yourself that the partnership can keep the rhythm going.

Ask students whether they paid more attention to themselves or to their partners. Was it hard to keep track of both yourself and your partner at the same time? Observe how long it takes before the students really catch on. This is a great opportunity to talk about learning curves for individuals as well as teams.

Source: Unknown. We first learned this activity from our good friend, Patrick Maurer (www.pmaurer.com).

Bumpin' Booties

Possible Themes: Honor/integrity, caring for each other, fun

Supplies: None

Physical Set-Up: Open Space

Do This

Have everyone get into groups of 4. Have each group face each other and form a small circle by linking arms.

Say This

With your group in its circle, you are ready to go out into the world to try and survive, or maybe even dominate! Your task will be to eliminate other groups. You will do that by "bumpin' booties." This means that when your group approaches another team with your booties out, you will seek to bump one or more of their booties so that you get a nice satisfying booty collapse (this happens when a person is forced to move their hips forward).

When you are able to collapse someone else's booty, then that person must turn around, relink arms with their group, and continue playing while now facing outward. A team can still move with one person facing out, but once two people have been bumped/collapsed then the team is immobilized and becomes an obstacle for other teams.

Now, before you begin, there are a couple of key rules!

1) *You are on the honor system for a booty bump. If you know you have been bumped, you must turn around.*

2) *There is a possibility that as someone bumps your booty, you also bump his, which is technically known as a "double booty bump." In this case BOTH of you need to turn around.*

3) *When two of your team members have been bumped and turned around, then your team is frozen. You must stay in place until we reset the activity.*

Okay, we are ready for action. Bring your group together, whisper your strategy. On your mark, get set, GO!

Give each round a time limit so that you keep things moving. A simple countdown from 10 will let the remaining teams know they are running out of time.

Once time runs out or there is only one group left, have everyone celebrate and then play another round if you have time!

Activity Notes: Cautionary note: this can quickly become a very active game! Make sure to monitor student's enthusiasm. Remind them to take care of each other.

In general, many groups are eliminated quickly, while a few groups can last forever. Observe how teams treat each other during this activity. Some will really protect their teammates, while others may have only a passing regard for those they are connected to. Consider highlighting the notion of honor and integrity. Students will often keep playing after they have been bumped. Understanding why they do that and what impact it has on both the activity and the group can be very powerful.

Source: The Boomerang Project

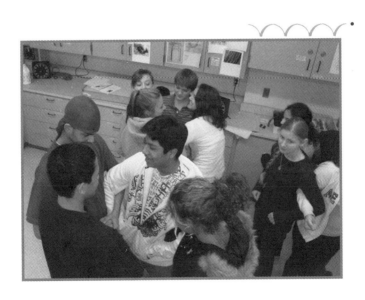

⌄˙Compound Words ⌄⌢⌢⌢·

Possible Themes: FUN!, trust, perseverance, honor, communication, icebreaker

Supplies: None

Physical Set-Up: Pairs

Do This	Have the entire class find partners and stand next to them in a large circle.

Say This	*You and your partner are going to decide on a compound word. As a reminder, a compound word is two words put together to form one word. You have 30 seconds to decide on a word and who will be which part of the word. For example: you might choose the word "toothpaste," with one of you being "tooth" and the other being "paste."*

Do This	Give partners 30 seconds to choose their words.

Say This	*Now that you have your word, you must create a celebration—a motion and sound to celebrate your successes. Your celebration must be something that the two of you do together when you successfully accomplish the task that is coming.*

Do This	Give partners 30 seconds to create their celebration.

Say This	*Everyone ready? On the count of 3, all partners say their compound word, with each person saying his/her own piece one at a time, and then doing your celebration. Ready, 1 – 2 – 3!*

And Say This	(Everyone says their word and celebrates simultaneously.) *Now say good-bye to your partner, and one of you go to this side of the room* (point to one side) *and the other go to this side of the room* (point to the other side of the room).
Do This	Students will now be standing in one of two unorganized groups on each side of the room.
Say This	*Now turn your backs to the other group, so you are all facing the nearest wall. Without looking at the other group, move around, mixing up your group. Your partner should no longer know where you are standing.* *Continue to avoid looking at the other group, and put up your protective bumpers. This is done by placing your arms and hands out in front of your shoulders with your elbows slightly bent* (demonstrate). *Now, keep your eyes closed throughout the following process: When I say "go," turn around and try to find your partner by calling out your half of your compound word. Continue to call out your half of the word, listen for your partner, and move toward each other. Once you have found your partner, you may open your eyes, do your celebration, and move off to the side to cheer on the other partners as they find each other. Ready, set, go!*
Do This	Continue until all partners have found each other.

Activity Notes: Establishing and maintaining safety, both physical and emotional, throughout this activity is important. Some students may become anxious with their eyes closed and all the noise. Also, when it gets down to the last couple of partners, do not allow students on the outside to laugh at them in a harmful way—keep it fun and encouraging!

Have the students think about what it felt like to be looking for their "other half" and what it felt like to find them. What causes the anxiety that some people feel in the search? Was anyone tempted to open their eyes? If so, why?

Source: The Boomerang Project. There are dozens of variations of this activity in many other publications.

Conversation Tag

Possible Themes: Tipping points, honor, groupthink, strategy, planning, logic/quick thinking, fun

Supplies: None

Physical Set-Up: Open Space

Do This
Have everyone make a large circle, standing shoulder to shoulder. If you do not have enough space for everyone to be in a circle, then make sure everyone stands where they can see you.

Say This
Each of you is going to choose a unique pose that you can walk around with. For instance, your pose could be as simple as the peace sign or flexed biceps. Your pose can move if you like—you could flap your arms.

Next you will name your pose—"Peace," "Strong Man," "Bird" and so on.

Your pose needs to be completely unique. So, everyone go ahead, strike your pose, and look around the room to see if you have duplicated someone else's pose. If so, just quietly adjust with that person so that your poses are now distinct from one another's.

Do This
Give the group 30 seconds to do this.

| Say This |

Okay, now that everyone has a pose, here is what is about to happen. When I say "go," each of you will try to appropriately tag as many people as possible, moving at the maximum speed of a fast walk. When you tag someone, you must shout out the name of your pose, converting them to your pose. Once tagged, you immediately adopt the pose of the person who tagged you.

Eventually, only one pose will survive! Whose will it be? Ready, set, go!

Activity Notes: Be sure to emphasize that the speed of this activity should be no more than a fast walk.

There are virtually limitless variations of this tag game. Break the large group into smaller groups and have each group get a specific pose. Play with the numbers and introduce additional constraints to see how that affects the rate of change among different poses. Notice the great conversation possibilities around how things change and the power of one person to make a huge difference. When playing this version with a group, get students to look at how ideas or attitudes can spread.

Source: The Boomerang Project

⌣ ˙Dollar Jump ⌣⌣⌣ ˙

Possible Themes: Things are sometimes harder than they seem, logic/
quick thinking

Supplies: A dollar bill

Physical Set-Up: Classroom

Do This | Set a dollar bill on the ground.

Say This | *I have set a dollar bill on the ground here at the front of the classroom. Anyone can try to win it. All you have to do is stand in front of the bill, grab your toes, and then jump over the dollar while holding onto your toes. If you let go of your toes then you don't get the dollar and someone else gets a try. Who would like to go first?*

Activity Notes: This activity looks really easy and turns out to be next to impossible. You may consider creating some build-up around this activity. For a few days beforehand, let students know that you are going to give them a great opportunity to get ahead. Give them the broad outline of the challenge, saying something like, "All you have to do is jump over a dollar." How many times in life are we given the broad outline, think "this will be easy," and then find out it is a lot more difficult than it looks? High school,

college, marriage, raising kids, earning an A, getting a job, finding happiness? These are things that are certainly not impossible, but many people find more challenges than they expect.

Source: *Silver Bullets* by Karl Rohnke.

Eyeball Tag

Possible Themes: Fun, energy, taking care of others, competition

Supplies: Chair for each student

Physical Set-Up: Chair circles of 10 to 15

Do This	Have students sit in a circle of chairs with one student standing in the middle (or you standing in the middle for explanation and to have some fun with them).

Say This	*I'm in the middle, and I want to provide one of you with the opportunity to be in the middle because it is a good place to be. So here's how you can get that opportunity.*
	Look around at the other people sitting in the circle. As you do this, attempt to lock eyes with one person. Once you have locked eyes with a person, you will change seats with him/her. As you get up to switch seats, I will try to grab one of your unoccupied seats. If I am able to get to an open chair, whoever is left without a chair is now the new person in the middle.
	Everyone can do this at the same time, so there will be a lot of movement. Be careful and take care of one another. Getting the open chair is the goal, but not a life and death situation— remember, if you don't get a chair, one will open up really soon. Let's start!

Activity Notes: First and foremost, there are some safety precautions to consider. You may want to make the rule that a hand on the chair claims occupancy in order to avoid major collisions. Also, remind them that this is a "challenge by choice" activity. If they don't want to participate, all they have to do is avoid locking eyes with anyone. That way they get to play without having to risk collision. They will still have a great time watching and laughing and will probably join in at some point.

This is a great activity to do just for fun. It is not necessary to have a conversation about what students learn every time you do an activity with them. In fact, that can take a fun activity and turn it into drudgery. It is okay to occasionally just laugh and have fun with each other! We give you permission!

Source: Unknown

Fast Fingers

Possible Themes: Thinking on your feet, strategy, influence, focus

Supplies: None

Physical Set-Up: Pairs

Do This

Have everyone get a partner. Have the partners face each other either standing or sitting.

Say This

Now that everyone has a partner, please put your hands behind your back. In a moment I am going to say, "Ready, set, go!" On the word "go," bring one hand out in front of you and display a certain number of fingers—for example: 3, 4, or none—it is up to you. Your partner will do the same thing at the same time. Once you can see the fingers on your and your partner's hands, add up the total number of displayed fingers as quickly as possible. Between you and your partner, the first one to say the total out loud is the winner. For instance, if you hold out 3 fingers and your partner holds out 4 fingers, then whoever says "seven" first wins.

Let's start with an easy round where each of you use only one hand. Any questions? Okay, ready, set, go!

Do This

Watch the students play a couple of rounds. If they look to you, just tell them to call out "ready, set, go" on their own and continue play. Once they get the hang of it, they are ready for the next challenge.

Say This

Okay, now that you have mastered one hand, I invite you to use both hands. This will be harder, but you can possibly think strategically! Ready, set, go!

Activity Notes: Play as many rounds of Fast Fingers as you want. Encourage students to think about the strategy they are using. Have them move around and play with multiple partners. You might even think about using different functions between the partners: multiply, add, square, etc.

It is interesting to ask the students to look at how hard that activity was even though the actual math was probably not very challenging. On their own, they can probably add 2 and 3 quite quickly. However, notice that they are much slower when playing with another person. Why is this? This can be a powerful tool in helping students see how much we influence each other, even when we are not trying to!

Source: Karl Rohnke. Not sure where this one is published, but we learned it from Karl.

Finger Fencing

Possible Themes: Competition/cooperation, different abilities, inequity

Supplies: None

Physical Set-Up: Pairs

Do This Have everyone get a partner. The partners should face each other, standing about an arm's length apart.

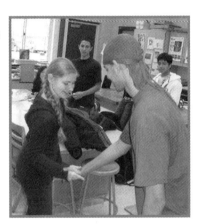

Say This *Facing your partner, take your right hand and make an L-shape with your thumb and forefinger. Now take your right hand and hook thumbs with your partner. Check to make sure your hand is locked with your index finger pointing at your partner. You are now ready. Score points by touching any part of your partner's body (other than his/her right arm). You must keep your thumbs engaged the whole time. When I say "En Guarde," begin trying to score points.*

Activity Notes: Set a short period of time, about 30 seconds, for each "round" of fencing. Maybe 3 rounds is a match. You could also change up partners each round, while having players keep track of their cumulative points.

Finger Fencing is a great example of a game that is fun for a very short period of time. Very quickly, students may notice that different natural abilities, heights, or strengths can make this game pretty one-sided. Others may find ways to compensate for their "disadvantages." How do they do this? You may even point out the fact that we all have different gifts and talents that give us advantages in many ways. Is that fair? Not fair? What is our responsibility when we realize we have an advantage over someone? How do circumstances change that responsibility? How does cooperating with each other change the activity?

Source: *Funn 'N Games* by Karl Rohnke, *Games of the World* by Mike Spiller.

Frogger

Possible Themes: Strategy, FUN, awareness

Supplies: None

Physical Set-Up: Pairs

Do This	Have everyone get a partner, and have partners face each other.

Say This

We are reviving an old video game called "Frogger." You and your partner will compete to see who can advance their "frog" forward. Just to be clear, the frog we are referring to will have to be in your mind's eye. If your frog can make 5 successful jumps, then it will be safe!

There are 4 basic motions to learn for this game. The first is with both index fingers pointing forward, this is the "advance" signal. The second is with both hands criss-crossing (like in the hand jive!), this is the "wait" signal. The third is with both hands crossed and touching your shoulders mummy-style, this is the "block" signal. The fourth motion is simply 2 claps.

Say This

Okay, using these basic motions, we will see which of you can advance your frog 5 times. Your frog attempts to jump forward whenever you make the fingers-pointing-forward sign. However, you cannot advance your frog when your opponent (partner) has the block sign up. Not only that, but your frog must always "wait" one time before it hops. You and your partner must keep the same rhythm as you play—2 claps, then 2 signs, then 2 claps, etc. For instance it might look like this:

Demonstrate the motions with a volunteer and then explain any advances.

**Do
This**

Partner 1	Partner 2
Clap, Clap	*Clap, Clap*
Wait, Wait	*Wait, Wait*
Clap, Clap	*Clap, Clap*
Block, Block	*Advance, Advance*
Clap, Clap	*Clap, Clap*
Advance, Advance	*Wait, Wait*

(Partner 1 advances once because he/she waited and then advanced without being blocked. After Partner 2 was blocked, he/she has to wait again before trying to advance again. Once you have waited, you can "hold" that wait and advance in the future, but you cannot store "waits." Waiting multiple times still only allows you to advance once.)

**Say
This**

Are there any questions? Remember, play until one of you is able to advance 5 times without being blocked—you'll need to remember your own hops. Let's give it a try.

Activity Notes: It may take students a few times to get the hang of this activity. Once the rhythm is figured out, everything gets a little easier. Although this is a great activity to "just play," it can also be good for talking about strategy. How did they plan advances? How much of a role does patience play? What's "blocking" them in their lives?

Source: The Boomerang Project. We have seen this activity under numerous other variations and names.

Gotcha

Possible Themes: Multi-tasking, focus/concentration, competition/
cooperation

Supplies: None

Physical Set-Up: Pairs or small groups

Do This | Have everyone get into pairs (small groups of almost any size will also work as long as they can stand in a circle).

Say This | *Stand facing your partner (or group). Place your left hand out in front of you with your palm facing up. Good. Now point your right index finger down into the center of your partner's left palm. Everyone should now have their left hand palm up and their right index finger pointing down into the center of their partner's palm. When I say the word "go," try to capture your partner's index finger with your left hand while trying to keep your right index finger from being captured! Go! Great, now reset your hands.*

Do This | Give the group time to reset their hands.

Say This | *Remember, every time you hear me say the word "go," then you are going to try to capture and escape, then reset your hands and wait for "go." Okay, so listen for the word "go." You might think I am going to count to 3 and then say "go!," but you don't have to wait for that. You can just go whenever you think it makes sense. (Keep talking and continue to insert the word "go" into your sentences in random and fun ways.)*

Activity Notes: This activity can be done in almost any size group as long as everyone can do both motions (grab with their left hand and escape with their right). You could even create a kind of Gotcha snake with students in rows. There are lots of variations available here.

This is a great activity for thinking about doing two things at once. Many people can focus on escaping or on capturing, but few can do both at the same time. What does this say about our real ability to multi-task? What are the consequences of offensive and defensive thinking?

Source: *Funn 'N Games* by Karl Rohnke, *Journey Toward the Caring Classroom* by Laurie Frank, *Adventure Education for the Classroom Community* by Laurie Frank and Ambrose Panico, *Games (& other stuff) for Teachers* by Chris Cavert and Laurie Frank.

Hand on Chin

Possible Themes: Behavior is more powerful than words, role modeling

Supplies: None

Physical Set-Up: Any

Do This | Stand in front of your group and follow the "Say This" instructions exactly, while demonstrating the motions.

Say This |
Take your right hand and stick it straight out in front of you. Straighten it completely so that you are locked at the elbow. Touch your thumb and forefinger together and straighten your other 3 fingers to make an "okay" sign. On the count of 3, do as I ask you to do. 1–2–3, put your hand on your chin. (As you say "put your hand on your chin" move your hand smoothly to your cheek.)

How many of you have your hand on your chin? Why did so many people put their hand on their cheek?

Try it with the other hand, that one might be a lot smarter! 1–2–3... put your hand on your chin. (Again, move your hand to your cheek.)

How many got your hand to your chin that time? What did you have to do to make sure your hand didn't go to your cheek?

Activity Notes: This is a quick and powerful activity to demonstrate the power of actions over words. Most students will put their hand on their cheek just as you demonstrated. Use this activity to talk about the power of actions versus words, the power of role modeling, and also the work that it takes to resist influence. For the last point, have them pay special attention to the fact that

they could put it on their chin, they just had to be aware of what was happening to them. This could make a great start to a lesson on media awareness, for example!

Source: Unknown

Hand Slap

Possible Themes: Predictable behavior, competition, anticipation, assumptions, observation

Supplies: None

Physical Set-Up: Pairs

Do This | Have each student get a partner and either sit or stand facing each other.

Say This | *Now that you are facing your partner, one partner will place both hands, palms up, toward your partner. The other partner will place hands, palms down, on top of your partner's palms. Everybody set? Okay, ready, set, go!*

Do This | Let them play for about 30 seconds to a minute. Observe their behavior. Very likely a vast majority of the group will play the game "slap hands." Some may not play or may play a different game, which is okay. Students may ask questions about what they are supposed to be doing. Just smile and wait for the processing to give them more information.

Activity Notes: The key to this activity is simply placing the partners in the appropriate set up, then giving them the "go" signal, and observing what happens. Whether students play "slap hands" or do nothing, you can have a very effective conversation about expectations and structure. One of the "maxims" we often use with this activity is "structure determines behavior." Because students are placed in a familiar structure, most of them behave predictably. Where else does this occur? Why does that happen? How can you use this?

Source: Unknown

Handshake

Possible Themes: Greeting others, mixing it up, taking risks

Supplies: None

Physical Set-Up: Large standing circle

Do This

Have the entire class stand in a circle with no furniture in the middle. Stand with the group as part of the circle, and actually go through the motions as you talk.

Say This

I am going to walk across the circle, approach someone, shake this person's hand, and say "Hi I'm ___insert name___." And this person will respond, "Hi ___insert name___, I'm ___insert name___. Nice to meet you."

Once I introduce myself to this person, we will switch places. That person will take my place in the circle, walk across the circle, and greet someone new. We will keep this going by continuing the process of approaching, shaking hands, introducing, and trading places with others in the circle.

Do This

Watch the students begin this activity, and then start a second string of introductions. There will be 2 people greeting at the same time. With a large group, you can continue this process, placing as many people in the center as you want. Some students may even continue to move and greet on their own.

When you've given this enough time, ask all the students to step back into the circle formation to stop movement.

Activity Notes: This is a great activity to get students mixing early in the year. It's also a good tool for mixing up a circle of students for whatever reason. If the students already know each other, just change the greeting/interaction. It will still mix them up.

Source: *Funn 'N Games* by Karl Rohnke. We first saw this activity at the Association for Experiential Education International Convention.

Matchface

Possible Themes: FUN, communication, comfort zones, connection

Supplies: None

Physical Set-Up: Pairs

Do This

Get students into pairs, and have them stand next to each other, facing you.

Say This

I am going to show you 3 motions and sounds:

First, throw both hands up over your head like a touchdown has been scored and yell, "Score." Let's do this together. Score!

Second, cross your arms in front of you like a genie, drop your head, blink your eyes, and say, "Bonk." Let's try it. Bonk.

Again, show me Score! Show me Bonk!

Third, turn sideways, kick up, and karate chop, showing your best martial arts move, and say "Hi-ya." Together. Hi-ya!

Show me Score! Show me Bonk! Show me Hi-ya!

Now that you know the motions and sounds, stand back to back with your partner. I will count to 3, and on 3, quickly turn to face your partner while doing one of the motions and sounds—Score, Bonk or Hi-ya. The object is to match your partner. So, without saying anything... shhhhhhhh... thinking about what you are going to do... sending a mental communication to your partner... ready, 1 – 2 – 3!

(Partners spring around and see if they match.)

If you match, give your partner a high five. If you don't match, shake your partner's hand and say, "My fault."

Now reset, back to back with your partner. Research has shown that if you determine who will be the sender of the motion and who will receive it, you will have greater success. So decide who is going to send and who is going to receive.

(Let them quickly decide.)

Okay, standing back-to-back, in complete silence, sender sending, receiver receiving... ready, 1 – 2 – 3!

(Partners spring around and see if they match.)

If you matched, give your partner a high five. If you didn't match, shake your partner's hand and say, "Your fault."

Last chance. Stand back to back with your partner. Complete focus... ready, 1 – 2 – 3!

If you matched, shake your partner's hand and say, "Great minds think alike!" If you did not match, shake your partner's hand and say, "Great minds think for themselves!"

Activity Notes: Matchface can work on a variety of levels. It is often used as an energizer with no other purpose than laughter and silliness. However, you can also have students notice their level of self-consciousness. The activity itself does not require students to "Go Big" with their movements, but it sure does make it a lot more fun. You may have students reflect on what holds them back from doing the movements 100%!

Source: *More New Games* by Andrew Fluegelman.

Old MacDonald

Possible Themes: FUN, taking risks, trust, inclusion, creating safety

Supplies: None

Physical Set-Up: Standing circles

Do This	Have students stand in circles of at least 10 (anything smaller than 10 is not as effective).

Say This	*Everyone put your hands out in front of you with both palms facing up toward the ceiling. Lift your right hand up, move it over to the right and place it down in the palm of the person standing to your right.* *I am going to start a tap that we will send around the circle.*

Do This	Take your right hand, cross it over your body and tap the up-turned hand of the person to your left. Then, pull your hand back and the person you just tapped taps the person to their left and this continues around the circle.

Say This	(As the tap is going around): *We want to see how fast we can get the tap around, so as soon as you're tapped, send it on.*

And Say This	(As soon as the tap gets back to you): *We are now going to add a song to this tap. We'll keep sending the tap around so be sure to put your right hand back into the palm of the person on your right after you tap. Once the tap gets going, I am going to start singing a song. I think you'll know the song, so join in when you recognize it, and I'll call the animal.*

Do This	Start the tap and begin singing Old MacDonald. The group sings and sends the tap around. Place whoever gets the last	Old McDonald had a farm, E-I-E-I-O And on that farm he had a cow, E-I-E-I-O With a moo moo here and a moo moo there Here a moo, there a moo, everywhere a moo moo Old McDonald had a farm, E-I-E-I-O

tap on the last O of E-I-E-I-O in the middle of the circle.

Say This	(Speaking to the person in the middle): *Okay, since the 'O' landed on you, you have the opportunity to celebrate. The normal celebration is that you get to spell your initials with your booty. But since you didn't know that and weren't prepared, we won't expect you to do that this time. So instead, give yourself a high five by clapping your hands up over your head.*

Do This	Send that person back into the circle. Now have the entire class practice spelling their initials with their booties. You must do it, too, and have fun with it. It is essential that you participate in this step in order to create safety. If the entire class is doing something a bit awkward together, they will laugh together instead of at one person. **(If you feel you need more safety, you can provide the option of spelling with their big toe.)**

Say This	*Okay, now that we know how to play and how to celebrate, we're going to begin again. The person on whom the tap landed last, will start the tap, we will all sing, and I will call the animal. Whoever the tap lands on this time, will go to the middle and spell their initials. The only other rule you need to know is that you cannot intentionally slow down the tap. You must move it along as fast as possible. Ready, start the tap.*
Do This	Play 3 or 4 rounds. (In a larger group, you can start more than one tap in order to increase involvement. Have multiple people, throughout the circle, start the tap at the same time. This will result in more people going to the middle, which is more fun and less threatening.)

Activity Notes: This is a great activity to help a group become more comfortable with each other. The action of spelling your initials with your booty has the great advantage of being perceived as high risk when, in actuality, it is low-risk. While it feels really scary, there is actually little chance that a student will do anything that will cause others to make fun of or embarrass him/her. If a number of people do this together, the risk is even lower. However, although the risk is relatively low, the benefit of the group sharing this experience together is high!

Many students will recognize this structure as one where they have sung a different song like "Down By the Banks" or something else. We recommend "Old McDonald" as it is more accessible to a wider range of students.

Source: Unknown

Pair Prayer

Possible Themes: Competition, spirit of play, focus, paying attention

Supplies: None

Physical Set-Up: Partners

Do This Have everyone find a partner. Have the partners face each other, standing a little less than one arm-length apart.

Say This *You and your partner are about to try to score points. In order to begin, I have to teach you the "reverse prayer" position. To do this, cross your arms in front and connect the backs of your open hands together. Now bring the tips of your fingers to your chin. When you are in this position, with the fingertips of both hands just barely touching your chin, then you are ready to go.*

When both partners are ready to go, then the game is on. If either of the players fingertips are no longer touching their chin, then the game is off. Practice for a moment moving from the ready to go position, to the off position. Okay, good.

Do This Give partners a moment to get situated and figure out the two fingertip positions.

Say This *When both of you are ready to start, the game is on. Either partner can try to score a point by reaching out with both hands and touching the other partner on both shoulders. The partner that touches shoulders first scores one point. You can try to block an attack. This can be done by quickly moving your hands away from your chin to block your partner from touching your shoulders.*

Both players have to be in the ready-to-go position before either one is allowed to reach out for the shoulder touch. A partner could choose not to play by never touching fingertips to chin. But how much fun would that be?

Okay, let's play. Everybody assume the reverse prayer position. On your mark, get set, GO!

Activity Notes: It is interesting to watch students make choices about whether or not they are ready. How much confidence do they have in themselves? How would you play Pair Prayer if you were really confident in your abilities? How would you play if you were not confident in your abilities? It is also interesting to note their attitude about competition. Some players may try cooperating to score points together. Note that nothing in the rules prevents this cooperation, although it certainly changes the activity!

Source: The Boomerang Project

Sidenote: Wouldn't it be cool if we had a national game? Just a quick, fun challenge you could issue to anyone with minimal discussion? We would like to officially nominate Pair Prayer as just such a game. Imagine being in an elevator with one other stranger. They seem nice enough, and you nod casually. Then you catch the gleam in their eye, notice the playful spirit of their smile, and casually ask, "Game on?" They smile and a 30 second competition begins. Well, we can dream anyway!

Quick Quiz

Possible Themes: Thinking outside the box, logic

Supplies: None

Physical Set-Up: Classroom

Do This | Have your list of questions (below) ready to read.

Say This

Okay, here come some pop quizzes.

1. *I will give (a dollar, bonus points, or early dismissal) to anyone who can put a piece of Hawaiian currency in my hand.*

   Answer: A U.S. coin or paper money.

2. *Who can give me the state with the most vowels?*

   Answer: Louisiana

3. *Which way do clocks spin in the Southern Hemisphere:*

   Answer: Clockwise

4. *Which state is the farthest west?*

   A: Hawaii

5. *Which country is closest to Russia, the United States or Canada?*

   A: U.S., because of Alaska

6. *Which weighs more: A pound of feathers or a pound of water?*

   A: They both weigh 1 pound.

7. *Where was President Abraham Lincoln when he delivered "The Gettysburg Address"?*

   A: Gettysburg (bonus points if students know that is in Pennsylvania!)

8. *Which city is the farthest west: Los Angeles, California, Spokane, Washington, or Reno, Nevada?*

   A: Reno, NV

Activity Notes: Quick quizzes can be used for a variety of different objectives. They can help introduce a topic that students think they know a lot about but maybe need a refresher. They can also be a great way to dismiss students when you don't want everyone leaving at once. You may even just want to pull these out at the beginning or end of class to get students' attention.

Source: The Boomerang Project. This is an adaptation from an activity we first saw done by Phil Boyte.

Screaming Ninjas

Possible Themes: Yes, and... Go Big and just fun energy, taking risks, caring for others, trust

Supplies: None

Physical Set-Up: Classroom

Do This | Have students stand shoulder to shoulder in circles of 8 to 12.

Say This | *You are all going to receive Ninja power. Everyone put your hands palm to palm in front of you and point to someone else in the circle. With that point, you can send your Ninja power to that person. But you cannot just quietly and easily send this ninja power. You must make a loud, powerful scream while simultaneously throwing the power at that person. Everyone try to throw your Ninja power to a few different people in the circle.*

Do This | You must demonstrate it with energy in order for them to get into it. Give everyone a chance to practice throwing their Ninja power.

Say This | *Now that you know how to send the Ninja power, you must also be ready to receive it. If I send the power to ___insert name___, he/she cannot reject it. This will help us model the "Yes, and" concept. "Yes, and" means that you are going to receive what comes at you AND you will pass it on. You must physically receive it, pulling it into your body, absorbing it as fully and completely as possible with both a motion and a sound. Go ahead, everyone practice receiving the power.*

Do This | Encourage the drama of accepting the power—be a good role model. Give everyone a chance to practice.

Say This | *Now that you know how to send and receive the power, let's start playing. I'll start by sending the Ninja power to someone, he/she will receive it and then send it to someone else. Let's see how powerful we can be as a group.*

Play for a couple minutes, encouraging creativity.

Okay, now we're ready for the advanced version. I will start it by sending the Ninja power to someone who will receive it. But in the advanced version, the person who is receiving the power needs the help of the people to his/her immediate right and left. These two people, one on each side of the receiver, will need to help bring the power into the receiver standing between them, physically and with sound. Then as the receiver begins to send the power to someone else, the helpers on either side must follow his/her lead and push the Ninja power toward the new receiver. So 3 people will be sending it to 1 person who will get the help from the people next to her/him, and it continues. Let's see how smoothly we can send the power around.

Activity Notes: This activity is more complicated to describe than it is to play. Once students get the idea, you will see a hysterical circle of screaming ninjas! Be patient as students get accustomed to "going big" with their motion and sound. As the group makes it safe for people to be silly, people will get progressively more silly. Your example in this activity is pivotal, you will set the model for how outlandish students can be as they send and receive the ninja power!

Source: The Boomerang Project. This was adapted from a camp game shown to us by one of our WEB participants.

Snoopy and The Red Baron

Possible Themes: Competition, creativity

Supplies: None

Physical Set-Up: Pairs

Do This

Have everyone get a partner, and then have partners face each other, standing about one arm-length apart.

Say This

You and your partner are about to take on roles. One of you will become a beloved cartoon character, while the other becomes his arch-nemesis. Are you ready?

Okay, choose one of you to be Snoopy and one of you to be his arch-nemesis, The Red Baron.

Now here is the set-up: Snoopy, in his guise as the World War I flying ace, was constantly having dog-fights with The Red Baron. To recreate this classic rivalry, each of you needs to place one hand in your pocket or behind your back. This hand is the airplane, and your pocket or behind your back is the airplane hanger. Your other hand simply does its best to stay away from the dog-fights.

On the word "engage," take your airplane (aka your hand) out of the hanger and try to knock your partner's airplane "out of the sky." The way that you knock your opponent out of the sky is by making contact with his/her airplane (hand). "Contact" is fingertip touching hand. The person whose fingertip makes contact with the other person's hand scores the point. Making contact with other parts of the body—wrists, forearms, etc.—does nothing! If a fingertip to fingertip contact occurs, both planes go down in flames with no points scored. Park your planes in their hangers and go again.

After a point is scored, the airplanes go back in the hangers. If you both agree to another dog-fight, say together, "Ready, set, go!" to launch the next classic battle.

Oh, and just to make it interesting, you may not move your feet at all during the activity!

Activity Notes: If players are having a great time with this, then encourage them to try a 4-plane dog fight, including both hands!

Watch the level of interest as students play this activity. They may quickly tire of trying to knock each other out of the skies. Encourage them to brainstorm about ways to increase the challenge of the activity! What are the boundaries for fair, competitive play? What rules ensure that both players are engaged, but no one has a distinct advantage over the other?

Source: *Silver Bullets* by Karl Rohnke.

⌣ᐧSpot Connect ⌒⌒⌒ᐧ

Possible Themes: Connections, ice breaker

Supplies: One-inch sticky dots (4 different colors optional), pens

Physical Set-Up: Open Space or Classroom

Do This

Have everyone take two sticky dots and draw one of 4 symbols on them: square, circle, triangle, or star—one symbol per dot. They may draw different symbols or the same one on each dot if they choose.

Say This

Place your sticky dots somewhere appropriate on your body: shoulder, back, head, knee, etc.

Now that you have placed your dots, listen carefully to the combinations that I call out and do your best to connect to someone else in the group! Your focus is on trying to stay connected to anyone around you, as long as you can reach them and you are touching the shape I call out! This is going to be a huge, room-size twister party! Ready:

Right hand to a triangle.

Left pinky to a square.

Right foot to a circle.

Left hip to a star.

Do This

Vary this pattern in any way that makes sense! Continue with a right arm connection of some sort, try a left foot or call a complete "release" of all connections and start fresh. Be aware that some connects might get tiring after a while.

Activity Notes: Doing this activity with colored dots makes the connections tougher by adding another dimension. For example, left hand to a yellow dot.

Not only is this activity a great icebreaker, but it can also be used to create groupings and get students talking to each other. For example, have everyone touch a specific shape, and then have the sub-groups that form begin a conversation on whatever topic.

Of course, you will want to ensure that students are behaving appropriately and maintaining their respect for others!

Source: *The More the Merrier* by Sam Sikes, Faith Evans and Chris Cavert. We learned this first at a workshop with Chris Cavert and Sam Sikes at the Association for Experiential Education Conference.

Toe Tap

Possible Themes: FUN, trust, perseverance, honor

Supplies: None

Physical Set-Up: Open Space

Do This	Have everyone get a partner (groups of 3 or 4 will also work).
Say This	*Please face your partner. Now, both partners place your hands on each other's shoulders—you should have both hands on your partner's shoulders. In just a moment, you will try to score as many points as possible in 30 seconds. Points are scored by using the toe area of your foot to touch the toe area of your partner's foot. You get no extra points for "stomping," so let's please use gentle taps.* (Similar shoes or both barefoot is a good courtesy rule). *On your mark, get set, go!*

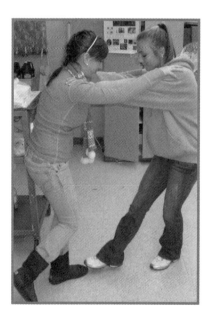

Activity Notes: The biggest concern about Toe Tap is people hurting each other unintentionally. Make sure you talk about safety and taking care of each other, and then watch the intensity fly! Also keep in mind that this activity can be both tiring and repetitive. Allowing 20 to 30 seconds is more than enough time for the participants to have fun and get the point.

Watch for the degree of competition that students bring to this activity. Many people choose to be either on the offense or defense and rarely change their strategy. Is that also how they deal with life?

As in other competitive activities in this book, you may notice that some people choose to collaborate instead. The rules do not specify that you have to compete, so some students may decide to cooperate by continually tapping each other's toes and collecting points. Is this good or bad? Is this more fun or less fun? Is this kind of cooperation more of what we should see in society or is it unrealistic? There is great potential here for powerful conversation.

Source: *More New Games* by Andrew Fluegelman.

Who Are You?

Possible Themes: Self-discovery, communication

Supplies: None

Physical Set-Up: Pairs

Do This

Have the group get into pairs. Make sure that each pair is facing each other and sitting either in chairs or on the floor.

Say This

In your partnership decide who is going to be first and who is going to be second. If you are the person going first, raise your hand. If you are the person going second, raise your hand. Okay, the person going first will simply ask his or her partner one question over and over. That question is: "Who are you?" The partner will respond with one-word answers. For instance:

> *Who are you?*
>
> *Brother.*
>
> *Who are you?*
>
> *Student.*
>
> *Who are you?*
>
> *Organized.*

The person going first will continue to ask the question until time is called. The person going second is responsible for answering each time with just one word, and answers can only be used once. For instance, once you say that you are a brother, you may not use that answer again.

When I call time, we will switch partners. Ready? Begin.

Do This

Give students about a minute to ask/answer the question before continuing.

Activity Notes: This activity is more powerful than it first appears. The process of trying to figure out who you are turns out to be a challenge. Students often find that while the first few words come quickly, it becomes more and more difficult as the activity progresses for them to name the different parts of who they are.

A variation of this activity is to have students alternate the "Who are you?" question with "What do you want?" The same one-word answer restriction applies.

This might seem like an icebreaker activity, but it often works more effectively with students who have already come to trust each other somewhat. We find that the answers are more honest and meaningful when students have a basis of trust to build upon. Pay special attention to the common themes that develop around who we are and what we want.

Who's Looking At You

Possible Themes: FUN, creative partnering, connections, observation

Supplies: None

Physical Set-Up: Standing Circles

Do This | Have students stand in circles of 10 to 12 (try to keep an even number in each group).

Say This | *Huddle up, huddle up!* (This should result in students putting their arms around each other, but each group will determine their own level of comfort.)

Everyone look at someone else's shoes in the circle. I am going to count to 3; on 3, quickly move your eyes from that person's shoes to his/her face. If that person is looking back at you, you have connected! High five that person, step out of the circle, and stand next to each other.

Those who didn't connect, huddle up again. Let's play again. Same rules. Look at someone's shoes. 1–2–3.

Do This | Continue until everyone has connected with someone else.

Activity Notes: This activity is often used to create partnerships for an upcoming activity. It can also be a fun way to get students laughing and connecting with each other. Variations of this activity emphasize elimination. The activities in this book do not focus on elimination. As a general rule, we believe that keeping people playing and making sure that everyone has fun is a more important objective than teaching students about elimination and exclusion.

Source: *Funn 'N Games* by Karl Rohnke, *Journey Toward the Caring Classroom* by Laurie Frank, *Adventure Education for the Classroom Community* by Laurie Frank and Ambrose Panico.

Who's the Leader?

Possible Themes: Observational skills, establishing leadership, creating followership

Supplies: None

Physical Set-Up: Classroom

Do This Gather students in a circle so everyone can see each other.

Say This *Today we're going to see if you can tell who the leader of this class is. We need a volunteer to go outside. While the volunteer is outside, we will decide on one person to be the leader. When the volunteer returns, we'll ask him or her to stand in the middle of the circle. Then the predetermined leader will begin a simple movement that the entire class will follow. The leader will change movements periodically, and the class will follow. The volunteer will get 3 guesses to try to discover the leader.*

Do This Choose a volunteer and send him/her out of the room. Have the class decide who will be the leader. Once the leader has been determined, bring the student back inside.

Once the student has returned, the leader covertly begins a movement and the others follow. The leader may change movements at any time; the others follow. The person who was outside tries to determine the "leader" by watching the movements change. If he/she doesn't name the leader in 3 guesses, the leader is revealed.

Do this activity 3 to 5 times, depending on the interest level.

Activity Notes: Focus your student's attention on what they were looking for when trying to determine the "leader." What do we look for in life to determine who leads? What distinguishes a leader from a follower?

An alternative to this activity is to give the class the instructions to begin a set of movements—each person in the class performing a different movement initially. Then have each person pick someone to "follow," and change to that person's movement. Although this theoretically means that all the students will be following someone different, many times they all end up doing the same motions. Does that mean there is a "prime" leader? How was that person established? Why was that person chosen?

Source: *The Incredible Indoor Games Book* by Bob Gregson, *Adventures in Peacemaking* by William Kreidler and Lisa Furlong.

Activities

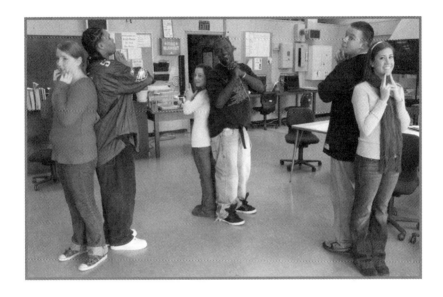

*It is in moments of feeling and excitement
that one's deepest lessons are learned.*
Wordsworth

Balancing Act

Possible Themes: Balance, change, competition, focus, harder than it looks

Supplies: Five dowel rods (one-inch diameter and 3 feet long)

Physical Set-Up: Classroom

Do This
Ask 5 students to come to the front of the class. Hand each student a dowel rod.

Say This
When I say "go," each of you will try to balance the dowel rod in the palm of your hand, making contact with only one of the ends. Like this.

(Give a quick example.)

You may not hold the dowel rod with your fingers at all. In fact, your palm must stay perfectly flat while the dowel is pointed up toward the ceiling.

The class will judge whether or not the participants are following the rules. Whoever is able to balance a dowel the longest goes on to the next round. Ready, go!

Do This
When each round finishes, invite 4 more participants to join the remaining student in trying to balance the dowels. Do as many rounds as you want if the student interest is there, or continue until everyone in the class has had an opportunity.

Activity Notes: Notice how the students achieve success. Generally, it is not with big, flashy movements, but rather with small, controlled ones. Isn't that how we often achieve balance in our own lives?

Students will inevitably see this as a competition, which is fine, but it is potentially very productive to shift the attention away from "who" was best to "how" people succeeded in doing it. It might be productive to have students list small ways they could increase their ability to "balance" their own priorities. "An ounce of prevention is better than a pound of intervention!"

Source: The Boomerang Project

Blind Goal Setting

Possible Themes: Goal setting, focusing on goals, observation, vision

Supplies: A paper ball, a pencil, and paper per pair (A paper ball is a piece of paper wadded up with some tape around it.)

Physical Set-Up: Pairs

Do This

Have everyone get a partner.

First, decide who will start as the thrower and who will start as the recorder. Throwers pick up a paper ball and recorders get a paper and pencil.

(Give them a minute to get ready.)

Next, decide what your target is going to be. Make sure your target is approximately 10 feet away from your standing position and is not much bigger than the size of the paper ball you are throwing.

(Give them time to decide.)

Say This

Now, throwers must keep their eyes closed as they throw. They have 10 tries to hit their chosen targets. The recorders will record how close each try comes to the target. Recorders may estimate each throw to within 6 inches.

Once throwers have made all 10 attempts, then switch positions. The recorders become the throwers and have 10 tries to hit the target.

Do This

Make sure there isn't too much crossover between pairs and their targets. After each person has had a try, start the second round as follows.

Say This Okay, let's repeat the exercise. The targets and directions remain the same, except this time you can keep your eyes open as you throw the ball at the target.

Do This Give everyone a chance to play through the round.

Say This Which attempt was more successful for you? How can we use this information?

Activity Notes: With paper balls flying all over the room, it can sometimes become too distracting. If necessary, be more specific about where each partner team should stand and which targets they should be aiming for— you might decide to hang designated sheets of paper around the room.

Obviously, the pairs should have much more success with their eyes open. Be careful not to make the point for them however! Using The 5 Questions model or other debriefing techniques, allow the students to come to their own conclusion. Although this activity may seem obvious, it is worth noting that our goals in life are not always clear or obvious. The metaphor of blindly throwing our actions out into the world, hoping we will hit something, certainly seems to apply to a majority of people!

Source: The Boomerang Project. There are dozens of variations on this theme that we have seen from a wide variety of sources.

Change Three Things

Possible Themes: Creativity, observational skills, adjusting to change
Supplies: None
Physical Set-Up: Pairs

Do This Have students find a partner. (Remember the fun and different ways you can partner from page 12!)

Say This *Take a few seconds to greet (meet) your partner.*

Now stand back-to-back with your partner without actually touching. And without peeking at your partner, change 3 things about your personal appearance. For example, remove a watch, pull up a pant leg, remove glasses, change your hair... anything that would be appropriate for the school setting.

Do This Give them about a minute, watching to make sure everyone is done.

Say This *Now turn and face each other. Can you find the 3 things your partner changed? Voice those changes to your partner to check your answers.*

Do This Give them time to find and check the changes.

Say This *Okay, leave those 3 things changed and again stand back-to-back with your partner. Now again, with no peeking, change 3 more things, making a total of 6 changes.*

Do This Repeat the process, adjusting the numbers, for 2 more rounds.

Activity Notes: Each round, the students will think that it is impossible to find 3 more changes to make, but don't let them off the hook. Push them! This is where their creativity kicks in as well as observational skills—they can see others making changes they can mimic. How do outside resources come into play?

Be careful not to give too much away, however. Let the students experience the struggle of coming up with what else they are going to change. The greatest creativity comes into play when they feel like they have nothing left to change.

Source: *More New Games* by Andrew Fluegelman, *Quicksilver* by Karl Rohnke and Steve Butler, *Journey Toward the Caring Classroom* by Laurie Frank, *Adventures in Peacemaking* by William Kreidler and Lisa Furlong.

Code Breakers

Possible Themes: Patterns, solving problems, creativity

Supplies: none

Physical Set-Up: Classroom

Do This
With everyone in the class seated, ask for a volunteer to be the code writer, and have that person come to the front of the room.

Say This
Okay, the code writer's job is to choose a specific group of people that fit a specific criteria, and ask each person in that group to come to the front of the class. The code writer will then arrange the group in a particular order, according to his or her code.

For example, a simple code might be tallest to shortest. However, the codes don't have to be visual. A code could be the sports that each person plays, arranged in alphabetical order. Be sure that the information to break your code is accessible to a majority of the class. Each code writer must use at least 4 people in his or her code, but not more than 8.

Your job as a class is to crack the code that is being used to choose and arrange those specific people. Whoever cracks the code can be the next code writer or choose someone else who has a code to crack.

Do This
Students may initially struggle to think of codes. However, as play continues, the codes will become increasingly more creative and complex. Make sure students do not create codes that only a few people in the class could know (for example, using middle names in alphabetical order that only a small group of friends might know).

Here are some suggestions in case students get stuck:

  Height
  Alphabet order of first or last name

- Sports
- Length of hair
- Shirt colors
- People who love baseball

Activity Notes: Encourage students to become aware of patterns. Finding and making sense of patterns is an incredibly powerful skill in a variety of disciplines. Essentially, students are putting together equations, and the rest of the class is trying to solve those equations. Resist the temptation to help the students too much (even though you may have a lot of fun trying to guess yourself!) The struggle should be part of the learning.

It might be interesting to ask students what they thought was more difficult, creating or solving the codes?

Source: The Boomerang Project

Creative Inventions

Possible Themes: Creativity, partnering, combining ideas

Supplies: A pen/pencil and blank paper for each person

Physical Set-Up: Pairs

Do This

Make sure everyone has a piece of paper and pen/pencil. Then have the students sit together with a partner.

Say This

At the top of your paper, write the name of an object—keep this to yourself for the moment. The object can be anything that can actually be seen and touched; for instance, bike, couch, orange, or book. Don't think too much about it, just write it. Once both you and your partner have written down your object, you can look at each other's papers.

Now your challenge is to combine the 2 objects to create a brand-new invention. You may not have to literally combine your objects together, but rather let your objects inspire your new inventions. For example, if one of you chose an orange and the other chose a bike, then possible inventions might be: an orange bike, a bike with an orange scented bell, fruit that rolls to you, a bike with wheels that look like oranges, etc. Your challenge as partners is to come up with at least 5 inventions!

Activity Notes: Do one or more rounds of this activity, switching partners to mix the group. Students tend to get better and more creative with each round. Encourage them to share their ideas that they thought were most creative.

Pay special attention to how far students allow their creativity to roam. Because there are very few external constraints in the set-up to this activity, it is interesting to watch how students put restrictions on themselves. Did they stick with the physical structure of the objects or were they able to let themselves be inspired by the "concept" of the object? Additionally, did they limit themselves to only the things that seemed "possible"? How would new things come into being if a few creative and bold individuals didn't take the time to envision the impossible?

Source: The Boomerang Project. This activity was distributed in the Focus Pamphlet produced by Phil Boyte.

Do What I Do, Do What I Did

Possible Themes: Concentration, focus, energy, role modeling, quick thinking

Supplies: None

Physical Set-Up: Classroom

Do This
Have all the students stand, and make sure you stand where everyone can see you.

Say This
We're going to see how well you can concentrate and focus today. I am going to begin an action. For example, I might put my hands out to the side and make small circles.

(Demonstrate this action.)

You will not mimic my action yet. Just keep your hands at your sides. Once I change my action, you will do the action I am doing now. For example, when I change from having my hands out to the side and making small circles to a fly-fishing motion (demonstrate this new action), you will begin doing my first motion with the circling hands while I do my second motion of fly-fishing. Then when I change to another motion, you will begin the fly-fishing motion. You will always be one motion behind me. Ready to begin?

Do This
Begin with a motion and continue to change motions. Make any motion you want, but it must be big enough for everyone to see. Potential motions:

Hula-hooping

Jumping jacks

Starting a lawn mower

Doing the backstroke

Touching toes

Be creative and have fun with the actions. We like to end with a clapping motion and then take a bow while the students clap for us—it gets a good laugh.

Activity Notes: This is a great activity for getting students really focused. The concentration and memory requirements make it hard to think about more than just the activity. It can also be a powerful activity for talking about role modeling and doing something different than you expect others to do.

To add difficulty, create more delays. For instance, instead of having the students do the activity that you just did, make them do the activity you did twice removed. For example, start with hula-hoop, go to jumping jacks, then go to the lawn mower. Students would jump in with hula hoop as you start lawn mower, then stay two activities behind as you continue to change!

Source: *The More the Merrier* by Sam Sikes, Faith Evans, and Chris Cavert (contributed by William Hazel).

Draw Me

Possible Themes: Learning from others, group work, dealing with change

Supplies: A copy of a picture (the more detailed the picture, the more challenging the activity), and a blank piece of paper and pen/ pencil for everyone

Physical Set-Up: Classroom

Do This — Have everyone sit at their desks and take out a pen/pencil and a blank piece of paper.

Say This —
In a moment, I am going to show the class a picture. You will only have 20 seconds to duplicate the drawing as closely as possible before I say "Time." You can begin anywhere you want on the drawing. Ready, begin!

(Show the picture for 20 seconds.)

Time! Okay, now please leave your drawing where it is, get out of your chair, and move forward one seat. Those of you in the front, please go to the back. You will now be working on the drawing that is in front of you, continuing where the last person left off. You have another 20 seconds. Ready, begin!

Do This — Repeat the process 5 or 6 times. Have students compare the pictures on their desk with those around them.

Activity Notes: This can be a fun activity for some students but frustrating for others. The challenge of starting something only to have to leave it in someone else's hands can drive true "type A" people crazy.

The challenge of this activity can be increased by not having a drawing in front of the class. Instead, have people start their own drawings, only to have others come in and change what they may have originally envisioned.

There is an interesting conversation waiting to happen around the idea of taking over what someone else has started. What is the balance between trying to honor what people have done before us and making our own unique contribution?

This activity works really well as a primer to group or team work.

Source: The Boomerang Project. *The More the Merrier* by Sam Sikes, Faith Evans, and Chris Cavert. This activity was distributed in the Focus Pamphlet produced by Phil Boyte.

Floor Paper Designs

Possible Themes: Working together, quality versus quantity, perspectives, solving problems, concentration

Supplies: 50 to 100 sheets of blank or recycled paper and a picture for your group to duplicate (use one of the pictures we have provided or create your own).

Physical Set-Up: Open space

Do This
Set-up a whiteboard or easel at one spot on the floor. Have the drawings that you will use prepared and in a place where the students can't see them.

Say This
In a moment, I am going to show you a picture. Your job, as a group, is to replicate this picture as best you can on the floor using the paper that I give you. You may not use any additional paper, but you may rip or fold this paper as necessary. Everyone must participate by placing at least one piece of paper. Please use only this section of the floor for your picture.

Do This
Show students the designated work area. It should be big enough to allow all of the student to move around the picture they are creating.

Say This
You have only 5 minutes to complete the design! Ready, go!

Activity Notes: Observe the degree of participation among the students and the attention to detail that the group exhibits. Who participated and to what extent? Why did some participate more than others? Did they work hard to make their pictures as accurate as possible, or did they settle for "close"?

Add some newspaper to the mix, and you'll gain some color opportunity. Please recycle the paper after the activity!

Source: The Boomerang Project. This activity was distributed in the Focus Pamphlet produced by Phil Boyte.

Picture Ideas for Floor Paper Designs Activity

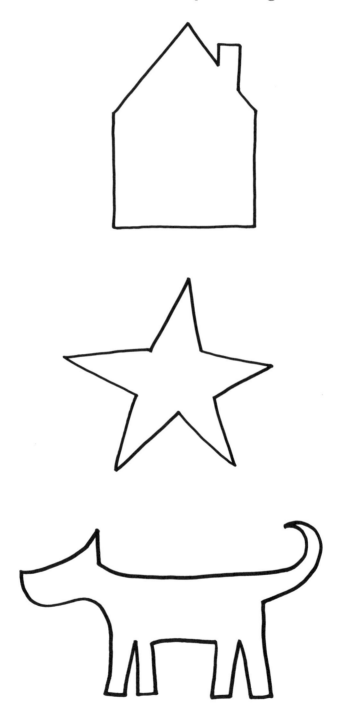

Gibberish Talk

Possible Themes: Balancing responsibilities, prioritizing, communication, creativity, fun

Supplies: None

Physical Set-Up: Pairs

Do This

Have everyone get a partner. Partners should sit, facing each other.

Say This

Today we are working on (communication, creativity, etc.). In your partnership, you need to decide who will be the #1 person and who will be the #2 person.

I am going to ask all the #1 persons to tell their partners a story. Choose any story you like, although if you have difficulty thinking of a good story to tell, then I recommend telling about your first trip to the zoo (or the dentist). If you can't remember exactly what happened, don't worry, your partner won't either—just make it up.

Now before you begin, there is a catch to how you can tell this story. You cannot use any language that you currently speak to tell it. That means you cannot speak English, Spanish, Swahili, Tagalog or any other known language. In fact, you cannot even use familiar sounds like "ooh" or "aahhh." Your challenge is to make up an entirely new language from scratch. It might sound like this: "Rackin splent formit scadua leeper, etc."

Okay, now that all the #1's have the idea, let's begin. You have 20 seconds. Ready, GO!

(20 seconds later)

Give all the #1 persons a hand! How many of you felt a little silly? Well, don't worry about that, because now it's the #2 persons' turn. Person #2, you are going to be even more enthusiastic than your partner—really go for it! Okay, #2 persons, you have 20 seconds to tell your story. Ready, go!

Activity Notes: The discussion following Gibberish Talk can go in a number of directions. The most important thing to remember about this activity is to model what you want from the participants first. Watching you be a little silly will give your students permission to be a little silly themselves.

Almost all students are inhibited in some way. Ask students what inhibited them. Why did they feel so silly? Why was it so hard to create a new language? They did it naturally at age 2. What happened since then?

Source: The Boomerang Project

Grab It!

Possible Themes: Communicating vision

Supplies: A paper ball for each pair

Physical Set-Up: Pairs

Do This

Have everyone get a partner. Have the partners find a space where they can throw the ball back and forth, with approximately 3 to 5 feet between them.

Say This

Now that you have a partner, decide which of you will be "the grabber" for the first round. The other partner will be "the thrower."

The grabbers should stand with their backs to the throwers about 3 to 5 feet apart. The throwers will toss the ball into the center of the grabbers' backs. The goal is for the grabbers to catch their ball without seeing the throwers release it—keeping their eyes forward. I will give you a few different ways to try this:

First: The throwers will toss the balls without saying anything, and the grabbers will just do their best to catch their ball. Grabbers, you will not know when the ball is coming, but do your best to catch it anyway. Do not turn around and look at the throwers at any time. Note how many successful catches your partnership makes in the next 60 seconds. Ready, go!

Do This

Let students try this method for a minute. Most of the grabbers will not be able to catch anything. If necessary, remind them not to turn around.

Say This

Time's up! This next time the throwers will toss the balls, saying "now" as they toss them. Grabbers will then know when the balls are being released. Let's see how many you can catch in the next 60 seconds. Begin.

Do This Let them try this method for a minute. Some pairs will be marginally more successful than they were the first round, other pairs will still struggle.

Say This *Time's up! Okay, for this round the throwers will toss the balls, saying "now" exactly when they think the grabbers should catch their ball. Let's see how well the grabbers can catch this time. The sixty seconds start NOW!*

Do This In this final round, a much higher success rate should be noticed among the pairs. Not only have the throwers had practice throwing, but communicating exactly when the grabber should catch the ball helps tremendously.

Say This *Time's up! How did everyone do that time?*

(Allow time for a little discussion.)

Now let's switch positions so that you all can experience the other role.

Activity Notes: Students are often frustrated by this activity. They really want to turn around and see the ball coming toward them. Encourage your participants to focus on just listening to the thrower and trying to catch the ball as best they can. This will give them the best chance for success.

In theory, the pairs will do better with each round. Help students understand how this relates to communicating goals and visions. The more clearly we communicate to others what is expected and what we hope to achieve, the more likely they are to accomplish those goals!

Source: The Boomerang Project

Human Etch-A-Sketch

Possible Themes: Empathy, communication, leading, following, anticipation, control, things are harder than they look

Supplies: Two pieces of paper and a pen/pencil per pair

Physical Set-Up: Pairs

Do This
Have students get with a partner and give each set of partners a piece of paper and a pen or pencil. They should be sitting together at one desk or a table.

Say This
Decide between the two of you who will be "Partner A" and who will be "Partner B."

(Give them a minute to decide.)

"A" will hold the writing utensil, and "B" will hold the paper. A will hold the writing utensil steady, in one position, with the tip on the paper and your elbow/forearm in contact with the desk. B will draw a picture by moving the paper underneath A's writing utensil. The only thing B can say to A is "Lift" or "Drop." "Lift" means that A should raise the writing utensil off the paper, while "Drop" means that A should bring it back down to the paper.

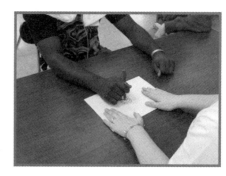

For the first round of drawing, the A's must keep their eyes closed. Now please close your eyes while I show the B's what to draw.

Do This
Write something on the board (or show them an object) that you want them to draw. It should be fairly simple but not too simple; for example, a face, a car, a flower, etc. Give them a couple of minutes to draw the picture.

Have them look at the final picture and talk about it.

Say This

A, what did you notice about having to be just the stationary pencil?

B, what did you notice about only being able to move the paper around instead of moving the writing utensil around like you usually do?

Do This

After some discussion, have the A's and B's switch roles, but this time everyone keeps their eyes open. All the other rules from the first round apply. (To save paper, use the other side of the first drawing.)

Activity Notes: This activity is an interesting twist on the expected. Many students find that just being the stationary pencil/pen is the most difficult role. Others notice how their sense of control is severely limited by moving the paper instead of the pen! Students can reflect on what it is like to be taken outside of their comfort zone or to play a role they are not used to. They may also have a lot to say about the difference between having their eyes open or closed during the 2 different rounds of the activity.

Source: The Boomerang Project

Loaded Down

Possible Themes: Stress, power of words, overextending, multi-tasking, vision

Supplies: 1 backpack/daypack, 4 or 5 large heavy books, masking tape, 5 blank pieces of paper

Physical Set-Up: Classroom

Do This
Have a volunteer come up front to help you. Instruct the volunteer to put on the empty backpack and go through a series of activities: jumping jacks; stepping up on a chair; sitting down, and getting back up; and/or walking briskly from one side of the room to the other.

Say This
(Speaking to the volunteer) *How did it feel to do these activities with an empty backpack on? Was it hard? Did the backpack have much effect on your ability to do the activities?*

Do This
Allow the volunteer to respond to the questions. Then, using Option #1 or Option #2, begin a discussion with the entire class.

Say This
We all carry around a backpack of sorts. It starts empty and then quickly fills with things we do or hear.

Option #1: For instance, we start the day ready to conquer the world, believing in ourselves. And then someone says something mean or calls us a name. What are some things we might hear?

Options #2: As we go through life we seem to get busier and busier. What are some of things that fill our schedules? What responsibilities do we have?

Do This

As students provide suggestions, write them on the blank pieces of paper (put more than one word on each piece if needed). Then tape the papers to the heavy books and put the books, one at a time, into the backpack that the volunteer is wearing.

For instance, responses to option #1 might include: stupid, lazy, dumb, etc.

For option #2, students may say things like: school, work, homework, sports, clubs, family, etc.

Check with the volunteer about how the backpack is feeling after each book is added.

Now have the volunteer do all the same activities that he/she did with the empty backpack, while wearing the backpack filled with books.

Say This

(Speaking to the volunteer) *How did it feel to do the activities with a full backpack? How was it different than having an empty backpack? How did it affect your performance?*

Thank you for volunteering! Give our volunteer a hand!

Activity Notes: This activity is great at highlighting the things that weigh students down. The discussion will go in different directions depending on how you set it up in the beginning. It should be fairly easy for students to identify the things that are weighing them down. It might be more difficult for them to assess what they can do about it. This is where you might want to spend the bulk of your discussion.

Source: The Boomerang Project

Make a Sentence

Possible Themes: Teamwork, creativity, the creative process, listening
Supplies: None
Physical Set-Up: Teams

Do This

Have everyone get into teams of 4, 5, or 6. Have each team stand in a separate circle.

Say This

I need one person in each circle to raise your hand and say, "I'll go first."

(Make sure all groups have identified who is going first.)

Okay, those people going first will start their groups by saying one word. To make it an easy start, the word must be an article like: "The," "A," or "An." Please choose one of those words.

Once the people going first have said their words, the persons to their right must supply the next word in the sentence. They can say anything they want, but it must make grammatical sense. For instance, if the first word is "The," the next word could be "cow." However you would not say "this" for the second word because that would make no sense. The next person will deliver the next word and so on.

When a sentence appears to be finished, the next person says "period" instead of saying a word. For example, your group has built the sentence, "The cow drank some water." The next person to add a word can say "period," and your group can then start the next sentence. Let's try this for about 2 minutes. People going first, get started!

Activity Notes: One of the most challenging aspects of this activity is getting started. Some students are inhibited and have a hard time coming up with words. This alone is a great observation to start a conversation.

It is also interesting to note what kind of authors they are collectively. Individuals are generally better writers than groups.

What does this say about the creative process? Are groups really smarter than individuals? In what circumstances might that be true or untrue?

Source: *Journey Toward the Caring Classroom* by Laurie Frank, *Teamwork and Teamplay* by Jim Cain and Barry Jolliff, *Adventure Education for the Classroom Community* by Laurie Frank and Ambrose Panico, The Boomerang Project.

Make 7 Make 11

Possible Themes: Cooperation, strategy, working together, ice-breaker

Supplies: None

Physical Set-Up: Teams of 2 or more

Do This Have the group get into partners. (This activity can really work with any size small group, but gets more difficult with teams larger than 5.)

Say This *Now that you are with your partner, please put your hands behind your back. In just a moment, I am going to say: "Ready, set," and then I will say a number. For instance, I might say, "Ready, set, 7!" At the moment you hear the number, each of you will bring both of your hands out in front of you and display a certain number of fingers without discussing that number with your partner.*

Your goal, without planning ahead, is for the total number of fingers displayed to add up to the number I call. So, if I call 7, and one person holds out 4 fingers while another holds out 3, then that would be a match because 4 and 3 equal 7.

The rule is that all fingers must be brought out for display at the exact same time, and no changes can be made. Just do your best to match.

Ready, set, 7!

Ready, set, 11!

Do This Play as many rounds as you like at this point. Then try the following addition.

Okay, now that you see how it works, I am going to give you a chance to improve. You have 30 seconds to strategize with your partner about how to be successful no matter what number I call. In other words, create a strategy for matching the called number, without talking or breaking the rules. I could call out literally any number, and you and your partner would be able to match it using your strategy. Got it? Okay, you have 30 seconds to create your strategies. Go!

(Give students 30 seconds to strategize.)

Time's up. Now, let's try it again. Ready, set, 3!

Ready, set, 17!

Ready, set, 32! What? Remember I said literally any number, right?

Activity Notes: This activity is great for highlighting any number of interesting dynamics. Have the students notice the success they had initially. Did they think logically about the patterns of their partners? Were their guesses "good," or did they just give up because they thought it was impossible?

It is also really interesting to talk about their strategy. How did they develop it? Who developed it? What happened when you called a number that went beyond the number of fingers they had between them? Were they able to deal with "any number"?

Source: Karl Rohnke. Not sure where this one is published, but we learned it from Karl.

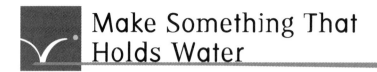

Make Something That Holds Water

Possible Themes: Creativity, using resources, achieving the impossible, logic, quality versus quantity

Supplies: One pitcher of water, an empty bowl big enough to hold all the water in the pitcher, and one plain piece of paper for each student (plus some extras).

Physical Set-Up: Classroom

Do This
Set the pitcher of water and the empty bowl on a table in front of the class. Give one piece of paper to each student.

Say This
Today we are going to practice some construction techniques. Using only the piece of paper you were given, and no other materials, make something that will hold water. Your creation must be able to hold water on its own. In other words, it doesn't count if it is really your hand holding the water with paper in between. The paper itself has to contain the water.

When you have finished your paper container, come to the front of the class and pour water from the pitcher into your container (holding it over the bowl in case it leaks).

If it holds water, great! If not, grab another piece of paper and try again.

If you were successful, share the information you have with others in the class so they can possibly do it too.

Activity Notes: Decide how many chances you want to give students to be successful. The hope is that at least one of the students finds success fairly quickly and shares that information with others in the class so that everyone can be successful. In this case, it can lead to a great conversation on sharing resources.

Students are sometimes tempted to give up and believe that this exercise is "impossible." Carefully observe the various reactions to this problem, and use that as a basis for talking about the student's perceptions of possibility.

Have fun experimenting with all the possible creations that will work! There are several different solutions.

Source: The Boomerang Project

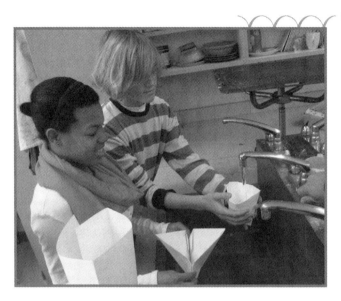

Perspective/Paradigm Shift

Possible Themes: Looking at things differently, open to new ideas
Supplies: None
Physical Set-Up: Classroom

Do This

Have students sit with nothing in their hands.

Say This

Everyone look up at the ceiling and imagine that you are looking at a traditional round clock that is placed on the ceiling right above you. Now, extend your right arm toward the ceiling and take your pointer finger (that would not be the middle finger) and point at the 12 on the imaginary clock.

(Demonstrate and have the group do this.)

Next, begin to move your pointer finger, along with your whole hand and arm, from 12 to 3 to 6 to 9 then back to 12. Keep moving your finger in that clockwise circle, going from 12 to 3 to 6 to 9 to 12.

(Repeat this a few times, guiding them through the circular motion).

Now as you continue this circular motion, slowly begin to lower your hand, still rotating, down and in front of your body, keeping your eyes on your hand and your finger pointing up to the ceiling.

(Continue to call out, 12, 3, 6, 9 to keep them focused on the clockwise rotation. Make sure everyone has this initial motion going.)

As your hand drops below your face toward your waist, keep looking at it, and you will notice that your finger is now rotating counterclockwise, 12:00, 9:00, 6:00, 3:00. It may help if you actually visualize another clock on the floor.

What changed to cause your hand to switch from moving in a clockwise rotation to a counter-clockwise rotation?

Activity Notes: Most students will be fascinated by this, and some will not get it. Just have those students who do get it show and explain until everyone gets it. Have them do it a few times.

What changes in this activity is your perspective. A rotation that looks clockwise when viewed from below will look counter-clockwise when viewed from above. It might be interesting for students to notice how many things in life are seen differently, depending on your point of view? Teacher versus student? Administrator versus student? Parent versus child? Help your students understand that they have a specific perspective, too!

Source: *Quicksilver* by Karl Rohnke and Steve Butler, *Power of One* by Maurie Lung, Gary Stauffer, and Tony Alvarez.

Playing Card Interviews

Possible Themes: Getting to know each other, discovery of diversity

Supplies: One deck of playing cards

Physical Set-Up: Classroom

Do This
Prepare the cards ahead of time, making sure the number of cards equals the number of participants. For example, create groups of 4 by using 4 cards from all 4 suits (i.e., all the 2's, 3's, 4's, and 5's from each of the 4 suits). A standard 52 card deck will supply 13 groups of 4. The number of students will very, but balance the groups as closely as possible. You could have groups of 3 or pairs, or even use multiple decks to create larger groups. The important thing is to have your cards prepared before you begin the activity.

Hand out a card to each student.

Say This
Do not look at your cards yet. When I say go, look at your card and then find 3 other people with the same suit (hearts, spades, clubs, or diamonds) that you have. Ready, go.

Do This
Allow time for the groups to form, then pose the following question. Fill in the space with what you want them to discuss—life, teaching, being a leader, etc.

Say This
Talk about what your suit says about your approach to _____?

Do This
Have participants share as a team and then share their teams' discoveries with the rest of the class.

Say This
Now, find 3 others with the same number that you have on your card (4 threes, 4 kings, 4 nines, etc.).

(Allow time for groups to reform.)

What values do you have in common with your team members? Come up with the same number of common values as

the number on your cards. If you have 5's on your cards, then discover 5 common values. (Aces = 1, and face cards = 10.)

Do This Again, have participants share as a team and then share their team's discoveries with the rest of the class.

Say This *Finally, find 3 others with different suits. Each group should end up with 1 heart, 1 club, 1 diamond, and 1 spade.*

(Allow time for groups to reform.)

Hearts: What is something or someone you love, and how did that love come to be?

Clubs: Talk about a time when you got "hit over the head," and how you came back from it.

Spades: Talk about a time you "dug yourself into a hole," and how you climbed out of it.

Diamonds: Talk about a shining moment from your life.

Activity Notes: If possible, have the instructions for the "different suits" groups posted or in a handout.

This activity can be used to talk about an endless list of topics. Using the cards is an easy way to establish the groupings and to start conversations.

Source: The Boomerang Project. Adapted from material in *Playing With A Full Deck* by Michelle Cummings.

 Robots

Possible Themes: Leadership, control, communication, fun

Supplies: None

Physical Set-Up: Open space

Do This Have students get into groups of 3 and spread out evenly around the room.

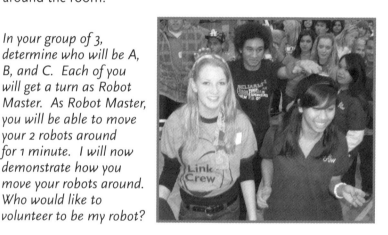

Say This *In your group of 3, determine who will be A, B, and C. Each of you will get a turn as Robot Master. As Robot Master, you will be able to move your 2 robots around for 1 minute. I will now demonstrate how you move your robots around. Who would like to volunteer to be my robot?*

Do This Have the volunteer come to the front and help you demonstrate the commands.

Say This *First, have your robot bring his or her arms and hands up into the bumper position to give them a little front-end protection. Now,*

> *One tap on the top of the robot's head moves it forward.*
>
> *One tap in the middle of the robot's back moves it backward.*
>
> *One tap on the robot's left shoulder turns it 90 degrees left.*
>
> *One tap on the robot's right shoulder turns it 90 degrees right.*
>
> *Two taps on the robot's head stops the robot.*

Do This
After stopping the volunteer robot, have students repeat the commands aloud with you. Have them repeat the commands to each other. Address any questions.

Say This
Now that you understand the commands, person A will have the first chance to be Robot Master. Position your 2 robots however you want to start them. You have 1 minute to move your 2 robots around the room. Is everyone ready? Go.

Do This
Repeat the process, giving B and C a turn at being Robot Master.

Activity Notes: This activity has the potential to reveal a lot about your students. An easy way to begin the conversation is simply to ask, "How was your turn at Robot Master like how you are as a human being?" Students often reveal a "dark" side of themselves by running their robots into walls, other people, or around in circles. What is it about control that seems to make us lose our sense of compassion? Resist the temptation to listen to those students who say that they were "just having fun." How many times are injustices done in the name of "fun" or "amusement"?

Source: *Journey Toward the Caring Classroom* by Laurie Frank, *Adventures in Peacemaking* by William Kreidler and Lisa Furlong, *Games (& other stuff) for Teachers* by Chris Cavert and Laurie Frank, *New Games for the Whole Family* by Dale LeFevre, *Power of One* by Maurie Lung, Gary Stauffer, and Tony Alvarez.

Say It, Do It

Possible Themes: Actions matching words, hypocrisy, honor

Supplies: None

Physical Set-Up: Classroom

Do This — Have students stand facing you. Demonstrate all of the following instructions with matching motions.

Say This — *Stand where you can see me. I will point my arms in a direction* (remember to demonstrate): *Up, down, or to one side or the other. When I point in any direction, you will mirror me by pointing your arms in the same direction. So if I point up, you point up and say, "Up." If I point down, you point down and say, "Down." If I point to this side* (point left), *you point the same direction and say the direction YOU are pointing which is "Right." If I point to this side* (point right), *you point the same direction and say the direction YOU are pointing, which is "Left." Ready to start? Let's try it.*

Do This — Go through the above motions, moving a little faster as they get the hang of it.

Say This — *Okay, you're ready for the next level of challenge. For this next round, when I point a direction, you will point the same direction as me, but SAY the OPPOSITE direction. For example, if I point down you would point down but say, "Up." Let's play this for a while.*

Do This — Play the second round, starting slowly to give them time to get the hang of it, then gradually speeding up.

Say This
Alright, now for the last challenge. For this round, you will point the opposite of the direction I am pointing and say the direction that I am pointing. If I point down, you point up and say, "Down." Ready?

Do This
Play this way awhile, starting slowly and gaining momentum.

Say This
Now that you understand the rules, I am going to up the ante on you. We're going to play each round, starting with the first one and then progressing. This time, though, if you make a mistake, you must sit down, eliminating yourself from the game. Let's start with the first round.

Do This
Quickly review round 1 and play it a short while, then review and play round 2, followed with round 3. **Do not play judge at any time.** The students decide when they have made a mistake and sit themselves down.

Activity Notes: This activity has a number of challenges. First, there is the difficulty of saying and doing different things simultaneously. This alone can be a topic of conversation that could take awhile! Second, you could have a great conversation about how the students judged their own actions. Were they honest about their mistakes? Without judging their behavior, you can easily get them to reflect on their own honesty and integrity.

Source: *The Game and Play Leaders Handbook* by Bill Michaelis and John O'Connell.

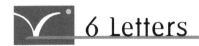

6 Letters

Possible Themes: Creativity, perspective

Supplies: Whiteboard, paper and pen for each student

Physical Set-Up: Classroom

Do This

Have each student take out a piece of paper and a writing utensil. On the board in front of the class, write the letters:

SBIAXLNAETNTAERSS

Say This

When I say "go," your task is to remove 6 letters from the letters I have written here in order to reveal a common English word. You do not need to rearrange the letters to make the word. You simply need to remove 6 letters and the remaining letters will become the word you're looking for.

Do This

Give the class a few minutes to struggle with this challenge. Notice how many give up on the task and the various ways the students try to solve the puzzle.

Activity Notes: The solution to this puzzle is to actually remove the letters "s-i-x-l-e-t-t-e-r-s." If you do that, the word "bananas" is left. The solution requires thinking about the problem in a different way.

Consider allowing students to struggle with this assignment overnight. Some will undoubtedly come up with the answer, in which case it can be very productive to ask them how they figured it out. Did they ask people? Did they research?

For those that do not figure it out, ask what they were thinking about and what prevented them from seeing the solution.

Source: *A Whack on the Side of the Head* by Roger von Oech.

Tap-a-Phone

Possible Themes: Memory, attention, communication, focus

Supplies: Paper and premade tap sequences (read the directions) for each team

Physical Set-Up: Classroom

Do This

Before beginning, write down different tapping combinations for the teams to use. This activity is like the telephone game many of us have played; however, instead of passing a whispered sentence along a line of participants, a tapping sequence is passed down the line.

Tapping involves using one's hand to tap another person, a tap being one touch. The group lines up single file with everyone facing forward. The person at the back of the line starts the tapping combination on the back of the person in front of him/her—tapping the back of head, back of head, back of head, center of back, left shoulder, left shoulder, right elbow. Use any body parts that are appropriate (depending on the level of comfort and maturity).

Have the students form teams of 5 or 6, and be prepared to pass out the tapping instructions.

Say This

Each team line up single file, facing forward. The teams should be parallel to each other. This game is like the telephone game that you have probably played before, except this time it will be done non-verbally. Do not talk at any time during this exercise. If anyone on your team makes a sound, your team is immediately disqualified. This is not a race, it is a challenge of memory, paying attention, and communicating clearly.

I am going to hand the last person in line on each team a piece of paper with tapping instructions on it. Do not look at the paper until I tell you to.

Once I give the okay, the people with the instructions will look at their papers. Then they will perform the tapping sequence on the person in front of them, in the order that it is written on the paper.

For example, "Left shoulder, right shoulder, right shoulder, center of back, top of head." So using their hand, they would tap (touch) the person in front of them once on the left shoulder, once on the right shoulder, once again on the right shoulder, etc., until the sequence is completed.

The person who was just tapped now performs the tap sequence they received on the person in front of them and so on, moving up the line of people until the last person receives the tapping sequence. That person must then write down the sequence, and we will see which teams were able to send the tapping sequence accurately. Do you have any questions? Ready? Go!

Do This

Play one round, starting with a few taps so they get the hang of the process. After each round, have the students rotate through the line, the front person coming to the back and everyone moving one slot forward.

Hand out new tapping instructions. (A variation could be to have the student write out his/her own sequence.)

After a handful of rounds, have a discussion around what was difficult to do in the process. What strategies did they use to be successful?

Activity Notes: There are a lot of variations to this activity that can change the message or the challenge level. For example, do this same activity in partners or have longer lines so that the challenge is greater. Challenge the entire class to accomplish the goal of sending the tap in exchange for something fun (or extra credit).

Of course, the most common conversation to have around this activity is how messages can change over time. What does this say about our memory or our ability to tell the simple truth? What does this say about how we communicate?

Source: *New Games for the Whole Family* by Dale LeFevre, *Adventure Education for the Classroom Community* by Laurie Frank and Ambrose Panico, *Journey Toward the Caring Classroom* by Laurie Frank, The Boomerang Project.

Tear It Up

Possible Themes: Communication, listening

Supplies: One piece of paper per student

Physical Set-Up: Classroom

Do This

Hand each participant a sheet of paper.

Say This

Place the paper on your desk. I am going to give you a series of directions to follow. You are not allowed to ask any questions or talk among yourselves. I will repeat each direction only twice, and I will not move to the next direction until everyone is ready.

First, close your eyes, and keep them closed throughout the entire activity, until I ask you to open them.

Now, fold your piece of paper in half and tear off the bottom left hand corner. Save this corner.

Fold the paper in thirds and tear off the upper right hand corner. Save this corner.

Ready? Last one. Fold the paper in half again and tear off the upper left hand corner. Save this corner.

Do This

When every participant is finished, have them open their eyes, unfold their papers, and compare results.

Activity Notes: The brilliant thing about this activity is how many different shapes will come from the same instructions. How was it possible that you could say one thing and they all ended up with different looking papers? Whose fault is it? Was there a miscommunication? What could you have done differently in giving the instructions? What could they have done differently in hearing the instructions? You could also ask where else this kind of situation occurs.

Source: *Quicksilver* by Karl Rohnke and Steve Butler.

Three Letter Body Parts

Possible Themes: Creative thinking, collaboration versus individual effort, knowing more than we think

Supplies: Paper and pen

Physical Set-Up: Classroom

Do This
Have students clear their desk for a test, and take out a blank piece of paper and a pen. On a whiteboard in front of the classroom write: "Create a list of 10 body parts with 3 letters in the correct spelling."

Say This
Okay, time for a test! Working on your own, create a list of 10 body parts that are spelled with only 3 letters. You may not work with your neighbor. You have 1 minute. Ready, go!

(After 1 minute)

Okay, who got 10 or more?

(Let them raise their hands; probably not too many.)

Raise your hand if you got 9? 8? 7? Didn't like this test? (That will be everyone who got 6 or fewer.)

Let's create our list together. Please raise your hand if you have a word on your list that isn't on the board. When I call on you, tell the class your word. I will write it on the board. We should celebrate together, so if someone says a word that you have written down, say "Oh, yes!" as we celebrate your genius. If you don't have the word on your list, let us know that as well by saying "Oh, no!" Then quickly add the new word to your list and no one will know the difference. Ready? Raise your hand to contribute the first word.

Do This
With the class working together, you should be able to easily get 10 words on the board. This will provide the foundation for your debrief.

Activity Notes: This is a great activity to open student's eyes to the value of collaboration. Working together has little to do with our intelligence and everything to do with our capacity to be inspired by others. Pay special attention to the fact that once students start to hear other's ideas, they will often find themselves coming up with more ideas themselves.

On a side note, be careful about the appropriateness of certain body parts with 3 letters. We leave it to your discretion and the sensitivity of your audience to deal with those situations!

Source: Unknown. We first saw this activity with Phil Boyte (www. philboyte.com)—further adaptations by The Boomerang Project.

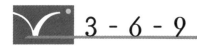

3 - 6 - 9

Possible Themes: Balancing responsibilities, prioritizing, observation, caring for others

Supplies: None

Physical Set-Up: Classroom, open space

Do This Have students stand randomly in an open area. They will play 3 rounds of the activity.

Say This *Each of you, without giving any indication, pick 1 person in this room that you will keep 3 feet from you at all times while you wander around the open area greeting and speaking to others. Do not let the person know that he/she is your "3-foot person." When I say go, create that 3-foot distance from the person you chose and maintain it as slyly as possible.*

Do This Invite students to wander around, greeting and speaking with other students for a minute or so.

Say This *Don't reveal your 3-foot person yet. Keep that person and add a "6-foot person," who you will keep at a 6-foot distance at all times. Continue maintaining the 3-foot distance with your 3-foot person. Do not reveal who either of these people are.*

Do This Again, have students wander around, greeting and speaking with other students for a minute or so.

Say This *Don't reveal your 3-foot person or your 6-foot person. Keep those people and add a "9-foot person," who you will keep at a 9-foot distance at all times, all the while maintaining the appropriate distances from your 3-foot person and your 6-foot person. Do not reveal who any of these people are. All 3 people are to be maintained simultaneously.*

Do This

- Give the students a minute or so to wander around and converse with others. By this point, it will be virtually impossible for people to maintain the appropriate distance from all 3 people.

Activity Notes: We all have 3–6–9 activities in our life: priorities that we want to keep focused on in different ways. How do students take care of all priorities equally? How do they decide what to focus on at any given moment? What type of balance do they achieve? It is helpful to make students aware of the fact that they were probably making a series of shifting decisions about which person to keep at the right distance at the right time.

Source: Teambuilding and Group Development, Learning Change.

Toothpaste

Possible Themes: The power of language, rumors, consequences, multi-tasking

Supplies: Two tubes of toothpaste (save on resources by using travel size tubes), 2 paper plates, paper towels for clean up

Physical Set-Up: Classroom, teams

Do This

Set up a paper plate and tube of toothpaste for each team at the front of the classroom. Divide the class into 2 teams.

Say This

Could I have a volunteer from each team come to the front of the class?

Each of you has a challenge. The challenge is to pick up the tube of toothpaste in front of you, take off the cap, and then squeeze the entire tube of toothpaste into the center of the paper plate in less than 30 seconds. Your team can cheer you on—as a matter of fact, they should cheer you on—let's hear some cheering! Are you all ready? On your mark, get set, GO!

Do This

Making sure the volunteers squeeze out all of the toothpaste.

Say This

Thank you for volunteering. You can have a seat. Team, give it up for your representative.

We need 2 more volunteers to represent their teams in the next level of the challenge. Please step to the front of the room.

Do This Wait for new volunteers to come to the front of the class, and have the teams cheer them on again.

Say This *Now your challenge is to get all of the toothpaste back into the tube. Since this will be a little more difficult than getting the toothpaste out, we are going to give you an entire minute. Teams, they are going to need your support, so cheer them on! Ready, set, GO!*

Do This Give them 1 minute to get as much of the toothpaste back into the tube as they can. Have paper towels available— this can get pretty messy!

Say This *Thank you for volunteering. Give it up for your representative. You can have a seat.*

Activity Notes: Obviously, getting the toothpaste out of the tube is much easier than getting it back in. In fact, getting the toothpaste back in is practically impossible! The following are some possible themes for students to focus on:

- Once we say something, it is very difficult to take it back.
- Once an opportunity is gone, it is difficult to relive it.
- Once you have an experience, or know something, it is very difficult to go back to a time when you did not know it.

Source: Unknown

Who In This Room?

Possible Themes: Perceptions
Supplies: List of "Who in This Room"
Physical Set-Up: Classroom

Do This
You could do this activity all at one time or use one question a day for a couple of weeks.

Say This
We are going to explore how we perceive each other. I will ask the questions one at a time, and you will write down the name of one person in this room in answer to each question. Your answers will be submitted anonymously, so let's have some fun.

Who in this room would you want as your doctor?

Who in this room would you want to go on vacation with?

Who in this room would you want to be stranded on a desert island with?

Who in this room would you want as president of the country?

Who in this room would you want to defend you in a trial?

Who in this room would you want to take a cross-country road trip with?

Who in this room would you want as your personal shopper?

Who in this room would you want to be the parent of?

Who in this room would you want to be your parent?

Who in this room would you want to be your brother or sister?

Who in this room would you like to trade places with for one day?

Who in this room would you want to get lost with?

Who in this room would you want at a party you were hosting?

Who in this room would you want to design your home?

Who in this room would you like to see act in a movie or play?

Do This   • Collect the pieces of paper with the names written on them.

Activity Notes: How you choose to reveal this information once you collect it is up to you. Often people just list a few of the top vote-getters and how many people selected them. You may want to review the list to make sure that all the students were represented in some way.

This activity works best later in the year, when students have had a change to get to know each other. It is also a good idea to talk to the students about the power of stereotyping. Did they just choose a friend or did they really think about the various personalities of the class?

Source: The Boomerang Project

Table 1: Possible Themes for Engagers

Engagers	Assumptions/Expectations	Communication/Connection	Competition/Cooperation	Creativity/Creative Thinking	Equity/Inclusion	Focus/Concentration	Fun/Energizing	Group Think	Honor/Integrity
Boom			◉			◉			
Bumpin' Booties						◉	◉	◉	
Compound Words		◉				◉		◉	
Conversion Tag						◉	◉	◉	
Dollar Jump	◉			◉					
Eyeball Tag			◉			◉			
Fast Fingers					◉				
Finger Fencing			◉	◉					
Frogger						◉			
Gotcha			◉		◉				
Hand on Chin									
Hand Slap	◉		◉						
Handshake									
Match Face		◉				◉			
Old MacDonald		◉		◉		◉			
Pair Prayer		◉				◉			
Quick Quizzes				◉		◉			
Screaming Ninjas						◉			
Snoopy & The Red Baron			◉	◉					
Spot Connect		◉							
Toe Tap						◉		◉	
Who Are You?		◉							
Who's Looking at You?		◉				◉			
Who's the Leaders?									

Icebreakers/Mixing	Influence	Leadership/Followership	Logic/Quick Thinking	Multi-Tasking	Observation/Listening	Perseverance	Risk Taking	Role Modeling	Self-Discovery	Safety/Caring for Others	Stratigizing/Planning	Trust/Comfort Zone
				●								
									●			
●					●							●
										●		
		●										
									●			
	●	●								●		
				●						●		
			●									
		●					●					
				●								
●						●						
											●	
						●				●		●
				●								
		●										
						●				●		●
●												
					●							●
								●				
				●								
		●		●								

Table 2: Possible Themes for Activities

Activities	Assumptions/Perspective	Change	Communication/Connection	Competition/Cooperation	Coping Skills/Problem-Solving	Creativity/Creative Thinking	Diversity	Empathy/Inclusion	Focus/Concentration
Balancing Act	◎	◎	◎						◎
Blind Goal Setting									◎
Change 3 Things		◎				◎			
Code Breakers					◎	◎			
Creative Inventions				◎		◎			
Do What I Do									◎
Draw Me		◎	◎						
Floor Paper Designs	◎				◎				◎
Gibberish Talk			◎			◎			
Grab It			◎						
Human Etch-a-Sketch	◎		◎		◎			◎	
Loaded Down			◎		◎				
Make a Sentence						◎			
Make 7 Make 11				◎					
Make Something... Water						◎			
Perspective-Paradigm Shift	◎					◎			
Playing Card Interviews							◎		
Remove 6 Letters	◎					◎			
Robots			◎		◎				
Say It, Do It	◎								
Tap-a-phone			◎						◎
Tear it Up			◎						
3 Letter Body Parts				◎		◎			
3-6-9					◎				
Toothpaste			◎						
Who in This Room	◎								

Fun/Energizing	Group Think	Honor/Integrity	Icebreakers/Mixing	Leadership/Followership	Logic/Quick Thinking	Multi-Tasking/Prioritizing	Observation/Listening	Quality vs Quantity	Role Models	Safety/Caring for Others	Stratigizing/Planning	Vision
						◉						◉
						◉						
◉				◉				◉				
	◉											
	◉						◉					
◉						◉						
												◉
			◉									
						◉				◉		◉
	◉					◉						
	◉	◉								◉		
				◉			◉					
			◉									
◉				◉								
		◉										
						◉						
						◉						
				◉								
					◉	◉			◉			
		◉			◉							
						◉						

Table 3: Physical Set Up for Engagers

Engagers	Classroom	Chair Circle	Open Space	Pairs	Standing Circle
Boom				◎	
Bumpin' Booties			◎		
Compound Words			◎		
Conversion Tag			◎		
Dollar Jump	◎				
Eyeball Tag					
Fast Fingers		◎			
Finger Fencing				◎	
Frogger				◎	
Gotcha				◎	
Hand on Chin	◎				
Hand Slap			◎		
Handshake					◎
Match Face			◎		
Old MacDonald					◎
Pair Prayer				◎	
Quick Quizzes	◎				
Screaming Ninjas					◎
Snoopy & The Red Baron				◎	
Spot Connect			◎		
Toe Tap			◎		
Who Are You?				◎	
Who's Looking at You?					◎
Who's the Leaders?		◎			

Table 4: Physical Set Up for Activities

Activities	Classroom	Open Space	Pairs	Teams
Balancing Act	◎			
Blind Goal Setting	◎			
Change 3 Things			◎	
Code Breakers	◎			
Creative Inventions			◎	
Do What I Do	◎			
Draw Me	◎			
Floor Paper Designs		◎		
Gibberish Talk			◎	
Grab It			◎	
Human Etch-a-Sketch	◎			
Loaded Down	◎			
Make a Sentence				◎
Make 7 Make 11	◎			
Make Something That Holds Water				◎
Perspective-Paradigm Shift	◎			
Playing Card Interviews		◎		
Remove 6 Letters	◎			
Robots		◎		
Say It, Do It	◎			
Tap-a-Phone		◎		
Tear it Up	◎			
3 Letter Body Parts	◎			
3-6-9		◎		
Toothpaste	◎			
Who in This Room	◎			

*The most extraordinary thing about really
good teachers is that they transcend accepted
educational methods.*

Margaret Mead

Appendix A: Partial List of Experiential-Based Learning Studies

Albanese, M. & Mitchell, S. (1993). Problem-based learning: A review of the literature on its outcomes and implementation issues. *Academic Medicine. 68(1)*, 52-81.

Delaney, Carol J. & Shafer, Francie Keller. (2007). Teaching to multiple intelligence by following a "slime trail." *Middle School Journal, 39*(1), 38-43.

Ives, Bob & Obenchain, Kathryn (2006). Experiential education in the classroom and academic outcomes: For those who want it all. *Journal of Experiential Education, 29*(1), 61-77.

Jowdy, Elizabeth J. (2006). An empirical investigation into the impact of an experience-based learning course on students' emotional competency. University of Massachusetts Amherst.

Laney, James D. (1993). Experiential versus experience-based learning and instruction. *Journal of Educational Research, 86*(4), 228-36.

Ruben, Brent D. (1999). Simulations, games, and experience-based learning: The quest for a new paradigm for teaching and learning. *Simulation & Gaming, 30*(4), 498-505.

Smart, Karl L. & Csapo, Nancy (2007). Learning by doing: Engaging students through learner-centered activities. *Business Communications Quarterly, 70*(4), 451-457.

Wurdinger, Scott, Haar, Jean, Hugg, Robert, & Bezon, Jennifer (2007). A qualitative study using project-based learning in a mainstream middle school. *Improving Schools, 10*(2), 150-161.

One looks back with appreciation to the brilliant teachers, but with gratitude to those who touch our human feelings. The curriculum is so much necessary raw material, but warmth is the vital element for the growing plant and for the soul of a child.

Carl Jung

References

Boyte, P., Jacobson, M., & Jones, R. (1997). *Focus: 36 ten minute lesson plans.* Meadow Vista, CA: Learning for Living.

Cain, J. & Jolliff, B. (1997). *Teamwork and teamplay.* Dubuque, IA: Kendall Hunt.

Cavert, C. & Frank, L. (1999). *Games (& other stuff) for teachers: Classroom activities that promote pro-social learning.* Bethany, OK: Wood N' Barnes Publishing.

Cummings, M. (2007). *Playing with a full deck: 52 team activities using a deck of cards!* Dubuque, IA: Kendall Hunt Publishing.

Fluegelman, A. (1981). *More new games.* The New Games Foundation, Headlands Press.

Frank, L. (2004). *Journey toward the caring classroom: Creating community in the classroom and beyond.* Bethany, OK: Wood N' Barnes Publishing.

Frank, L. & Panico, A. (2000, 2007). *Adventure education for the classroom community.* Bloomington, IN: Solution Tree.

Gregson, B. (1982). *The incredible indoor games book.* Belmont, CA: David S. Lake, Publisher.

Inspire: Ice Breakers and Openers (CD-ROM, 2003). Chico, CA: Learning Change.

Jacobson, M. & Ruddy, M. (2004). *Open to outcome: A practical guide for facilitating and teaching experiential reflection.* Bethany, OK: Wood N' Barnes Publishing.

Kreidler, W. J. & Furlong, L. (1996). *Adventures in peacemaking: A conflict resolution activity guide.* Cambridge, MA: Educators for Social Responsibility & Project Adventure, Inc.

LeFevre, D. (1988). *New games for the whole family.* The New Games Foundation, Headlands Press.

Lung, M., Stauffer, G., & Alvarez, T. (2008). *Power of one: Using adventure and experiential activities within one on one counseling sessions.* Bethany, OK: Wood N' Barnes Publishing.

Michaelis, B. & O'Connell, J. M. (2000). *The game and play leaders handbook: Facilitating fun and positive interaction.* State College, PA: Venture.

Rohnke, K. (1984). *Silver bullets: A guide to initiative problems, adventure, games and trust activities.* Dubuque, IA: Kendall Hunt.

Rohnke, K. (2004). *The bottomless bag revival! (revised 2nd ed.)* Dubuque, IA: Kendall Hunt.

Rohnke, K. (2004). *Funn 'n games: Adventure games, initiatives, and trust activities for fun and facilitation.* Dubuque, IA: Kendall Hunt.

Rohnke, K. & Bulter, S. (1995). *Quicksilver: Adventure games, initiative problems, trust activities, and a guide to effective leadership.* Dubuque, IA: Kendall Hunt.

Stanchfield, J. (2007). *Tips and tools: The art of experiential group facilitation.* Bethany, OK: Wood N' Barnes Publishing.

Sikes, S., Evans, F., & Cavert, C. (2007). *The more the merrier: Lead playful activities with large groups.* DoingWorks Publishing.

Simpson, S., Miller, D., & Bocher, B. (2006). *The processing pinnacle: An educator's guide to better processing.* Bethany, OK: Wood N' Barnes Publishing.

Teambuilding and Group Development (CD-ROM, 2006). Chico, CA: Learning Change.

von Oech, R. (1990). *A whack on the side of the head: How you can be more creative, rev. ed.* NY: Grand Central Publishing.

The Authors
Micah, Carolyn & Mary Beth

MARY BETH CAMPBELL is the Boomerang Project's chief visionary who is deeply and sincerely passionate about making the world a better place. Her far-reaching talents, which include an extraordinary singing voice and a nearly limitless supply of exciting new creative concepts, are only superseded by her personal standards of excellence.

A graduate of San Diego State with a degree in English, Mary Beth was an exceptional high school English teacher and ran an award-winning journalism program before her work with Link Crew. She directed the highly successful student transition program at her high school for five years. During that period, she discovered the profoundly life-changing value of Link Crew and saw the possibility of how it could transform even the most challenged educational setting.

After leaving the classroom, Mary Beth became a lead trainer for both Link Crew and WEB, the WEB Program Director as well as the company's Marketing Director. Her tenacity and focus has helped double the size of the Boomerang Project outreach and she is now developing new line of exciting social responsibility products, which will be marketed to both consumers and schools.

CAROLYN HILL: After 15 years motivating and transforming students as a highly respected English teacher and an Activities Director, Carolyn did what she never imagined doing: she left the classroom and joined the Boomerang Project. The impetus for this decision was her attendance at the very first Link Crew training in 1992. After implementing the program at two different schools, and seeing the dramatic impact it could have creating an exciting new spirit of success among students, she wanted every school to have access to such an innovative transition model.

Carolyn began her full-time work with the Boomerang Project in 1999 as the Link Crew Program Director, providing critical consulting perspective and an ability to identify solutions for the real challenges faced by schools across the country. Carolyn earned her BA from UCSB and her Masters in Education from San Jose State. Her insightful teaching skills and extensive classroom experience have been invaluable in her role as a lead trainer. Feedback from years of workshops repeatedly praises Carolyn's intuitive gifts, her capacity for connecting deeply with others and igniting their enthusiasm with her own.

MICAH JACOBSON: Co-founder of The Boomerang Project, Micah has helped empower thousands of schools across the country to improve the transition process for new students by providing a toolbox of new character development resources geared to build a sense of community and a culture of success. A dynamic, passionate presenter, Micah has been a lead trainer for the innovative Link Crew and WEB student transition programs since 1992. Link Crew and WEB are now used in over 2300 schools reaching more than 1 million students every year in 41 US states and 4 Canadian Provinces.

Micah holds BA degrees in Politics, Philosophy and Economics from Claremont McKenna College and earned an MBA from the University of Michigan. He has co-authored four books, including *Open to Outcome: A Practical Guide to Teaching and Facilitating Experiential Reflection*, a book that was nominated as a top 10 education book of the year by Forward Magazine.

A sought-after, highly engaging speaker, he makes frequent appearances at leading education conferences around the world, sharing his perspectives on the ethics of reciprocity, experiential learning and the complex issues of school transition. During the last 10 years, Micah has also extended his professional training internationally in Russia, Brazil, Israel and Tanzania. He was a trainer with the United Nations Global Youth Forum, and was selected as a Youth Trainer at two Global Youth Summits.

Contact Information:
Phone: 831.460.7040 800.688.7578
www.boomerangproject.com
info@boomerangproject.com